WORLD WAR II
FURY IN THE PACIFIC

WORLD WAR II
FURY IN THE PACIFIC

Published by Bookmart Ltd 2005

Blaby Road,
Wigson,
Leicester,
LE18 4SE
Books@bookmart.co.uk

Copyright ©2005 Taj Books Ltd

All notations of errors or omissions (author inquiries, permissions) concerning the content of this book should be addressed to TAJ Books 27, Ferndown Gardens, Cobham, Surrey, UK, KT11 2BH, info@tajbooks.com.

ISBN 1-84509-172-8

Printed in China.
1 2 3 4 5 08 07 06 05

CONTENTS

Admiral Osami Nagano Ijn Chief of the Naval General Staff.

On July 2, 1941, the Imperial Council of Japan decided to avail itself at once of the opportunity it now had to extend Japanese dominion over the whole of Indo-China; and on July 14, Kato, Japanese Ambassador in Paris, informed Admiral Darlan, then head of the Vichy Government, of a request to this effect from the Prime Minister, Prince Konoye. It was a case of organising the "joint defence" of the colony and this, Tokyo asserted, involved its entire occupation by an unlimited number of troops and, in addition, the right for the occupying force to set up bases wherever it pleased.

Within 24 hours, Darlan alerted Admiral Leahy, United States Ambassador in the capital of Unoccupied France. But from documents which have been published on the subject, it appears that, while encouraging Darlan and Marshal Pétain to resist this pressure on the part of Tokyo, Leahy, contrary to reliable sources of information, gave them no effective guarantee of aid in the eventuality of French intransigence resulting in the invasion of Indo-China.

According to the wording of a memorandum from Vichy to Washington, dated August 5, President Roosevelt's Ambassador, earlier on July 16, "in the course of conversations with Marshal Pétain informed him that there were no grounds for thinking that the American Government was disposed to reconsider the passive attitude adopted by the State Department following the first Japanese intervention in 1940."

In these conditions, Vichy bowed to the inevitable, and on July 29, 1941 an exchange of letters between Kato and Darlan ratified the agreement which had been signed in Hanoi by Admiral

Decoux and the Japanese negotiators.

Just when Prince Konoye was trying to come to an agreement with Washington, and had in fact, in the hope of a settlement, sacrificed Matsuoka and installed Admiral Toyoda in his place, the news of the occupation of Saigon hit the United States with the force of a thunderbolt and obviated all Konoye's efforts.

And, indeed, if the establishment of Japanese bases in Cochin-China hardly constituted an act of war, it was none theless an act preparatory to war which threatened at one and the same time the British positions in Burma and Malaya, the Dutch in Indonesia, and the American in the Philippines. President Roosevelt's reaction was to freeze Japanese assets in the United States as from July 26 and to place an embargo on exports of oil to Japan. A few days later, the United Kingdom, Canada, and the Dutch Government in exile followed suit, thus straightway depriving Japan of any access to the Sumatra, Borneo, and Burma oilfields.

Negotiations with the United States

Nevertheless, these new developments had no effect on the Japanese Government's attempts to restart negotiations, and, as has already been observed, President Roosevelt, who wanted to give his British allies time to strengthen Singapore, was not unwilling to talk. To this end, Prince Konoye proposed a meeting with President Roosevelt in Honolulu, but he was informed by Washington that it was desirable first to prepare the ground by diplomatic negotiation.

And indeed, with the embargo on oil, Franklin Roosevelt and Cordell Hull possessed a most effective means of exerting

Map of positions of US warships docked at Pearl Harbor.

pressure, since it was estimated that Japanese stocks of oil would not last more than two years. But, in fact, this was a double-edged weapon; for it was idle to think that the exchange of diplomatic notes between Tokyo and Washington would be allowed to continue indefinitely at a time when the fleet of the Rising Sun might find itself incapacitated for lack of fuel oil. Especially when Tarakan and Balikpapan in Borneo and Palembang in Sumatra, not to mention the Burmese installations of Burmah Oil, might all be within striking distance. And so, Japan's military leaders, without rejecting attempts to obtain a negotiated settlement out of hand, insisted on a time limit being set to the negotiations, for it would not do to submit to the considerable advantage the other

Japan Navy - crew on aircraft carrier cheer departing Nakajim B5N 'Kate' torpedo.

party would obtain, if negotiations were broken off, simply by constant temporising.

On September 6, upon the covert refusal of President Roosevelt to meet the Japanese Prime Minister either in Honolulu or even in Juneau (Alaska), the Imperial Council met again to consider the situation; there was no avoiding the arguments that

have just been summarised and the following conclusions were drawn:

1. Japan, "determined not to reject the possibility of a conflict", was likely to have completed her preparations for war between that time and the end of October;

2. "Parallel to and in tune with this", she would endeavour, "by all diplomatic means", to reach agreement with the United States and Great Britain on the basis of the programme which had been

drawn up in Tokyo; and

3. "If, at the beginning of October, there was no longer any appearance of our demands being able to be met by means of negotiation, it would be resolved to go to war with the United States, Great Britain, and the Netherlands."

Accordingly, while the Japanese Foreign Minister was informing Ambassador Grew of his government's intentions, Admiral Nomura, the Japanese Ambassador in Washington, was conveying them on September-28 to Secretary of State Cordell Hull, who gave him a somewhat cold reception as it transpired from a reading of his memorandum of October 2.

The military gain the upper hand

The date fixed by the Imperial Council on September 6 passed with absolutely no solution to the diplomatic impasse and, on October 12, Prince Konoye summoned his Minister of Foreign Affairs, Admiral Toyoda, War Minister, General Tojo Navy Minister, Admiral Okawa, and General Suzuki, the head of military planning, to his villa on the outskirts of Tokyo. According to the account of this meeting which has come down to us from Giuglaris, words ran high between the head of the Japanese Government and his Minister of War:

Tojo: "Negotiations cannot succeed. In order for them to succeed, there must be concessions on both sides. Till now, it is Japan that has made the concessions, the Americans who have not budged an inch."

Okawa: "We're precisely balanced between peace and war. It is up to the Prime Minister to decide and to stand by his decision."

Tojo: "It's not as simple as that. It's not the Prime Minister

alone who counts, there are the army and the navy."

Konoye: "We can contemplate a one- or two-year war with equanimity, but not so a war that might last more than two years."

Tojo: "That reflection is the Prime Minister's personal opinion."

Konoye: "I would rather a diplomatic solution than war."

Tojo: "The question of the Prime Minister's confidence in going to war should have been discussed in the Imperial Council. The Prime Minister attended that Council, did he not? There can be no question now of his evading his responsibilities."

Konoye: "Not only do I have no confidence in going to war but I refuse to take responsibility for doing so. The only action taken by the Imperial Council was to determine the measures to be taken should all diplomatic means fail. I still have confidence in a diplomatic solution."

With the benefit of the hindsight afforded the historian as compared with those who direct the course of events, one is at liberty to point out that both men were wrong on October 12, 1941. General Hideki Tojo was in error in assuming that, given the maximum effect of surprise, the military potential of the Japanese Empire would in one fell swoop inflict a fatal blow on the American colossus. And, on his side, Prince Fumimaro Konoye was under a delusion in thinking that the country with which he was trying to reach agreement, invigorated by the anticipated effect of the oil embargo she had imposed, would lift it merely for Japan's assurance not to use Indo-China as a springboard for the conquest of South-East Asia.

Be that as it may, General Tojo was uttering no empty threat when he called his Prime Minister's attention to the state of opinion in the Army and the Navy, for, under the terms of the Japanese constitution, the ministers responsible for national defence were appointed by the Emperor and so escaped the rule of ministerial solidarity, and could at any time within the cabinet voice the censure of the military. In which case, the Prime Minister must tender his resignation; this in effect occurred on October 16, 1941, the instigator of the crisis then being called upon to resolve it.

The United States still remain unworried

At the time, this latest ministerial crisis in Japan caused no disquiet in the American Embassy in Tokyo; the military attaché, Lieutenant-Colonel Cresswell, commenting on the fact, wrote to the Secretary for War: "The composition of the new government is the very image of conservatism, but it is not thought that the resignation of the government led by Konoye will mark an abrupt change, at least not for the present. Certainly, General Tojo puts Japan before all else, but he is said to have a breadth of view which goes against his embarking on an extreme course."

Instancing the Emperor's pressing for a peaceful settlement, Ambassador Grew held approximately the same view as his military attaché. Nevertheless, on November 3, he put Secretary of State Cordell Hull on guard against imagining that Tojo would direct his conduct according to the norms of self-interest generally accepted in the West. "Make no mistake," he cabled, "the Japanese are capable of launching a suicide war with the United States. Self-interest should prevent them doing so; but Japanese national self-interest cannot be assessed according to the canons of our logic." The new Minister of Foreign Affairs in the Tojo Cabinet declared his earnest intention of enabling negotiations between Japan and America to succeed as soon as he took up office, and, on October 20, his Prime Minister declared that the maintenance of world peace was the first concern of his government's policy. But time was running out: throughout the Empire, stocks of liquid fuel were dwindling slowly but surely; moreover, the weather conditions prevailing in South-East Asia argued for action before December 15. The military necessities of the situation were now forcing the politicians' hands.

Admiral Isoroku Yamamoto was C.-in-C. of the Imperial Japanese Navy when war came in 1941. Born in 1884, he was no stranger to the United States. He had studied at Harvard and had served in the U.S.A. as a naval attaché. He was one of the first "air-minded" naval strategists of the 20th Century, and had been instrumental in seeing to it that the powerful Japanese Combined Fleet was equipped with a strong force of aircraft-carriers. Faced with the pressure for war with the United States which came from the army leaders, Yamamoto always argued that in the long run Japan must lose any protracted war because her industrial potential could not match that of the Americans. When he was argued down he based his naval strategy on swift, knock-out blows, of which the first and most important was the attack on Pearl Harbor to annihilate the U.S. Pacific Fleet. Despite the brilliant successes gained at Pearl Harbor, and the fact that by January 1942 every Allied battleship in the Pacific was out of action or sunk, Yamamoto's basic plan had not succeeded: the

Japan Navy - aircraft on carrier prior to attack on Pearl Harbor.

all-important American carrier fleet in the Pacific escaped to fight again.

The U.S. conditions

The last stipulation in the Japanese offer of November 20 was in fact unacceptable to the government and public opinion in America. But the counter-proposals for a modus vivendi that Cordell Hull handed to the two envoys, Kurusu and Nomura, on November 26, were for Japan still more unacceptable: the American Secretary of State posed as a prerequisite the evacuation not only of Indo-China, but of all China, the disowning of the puppet governments in Mukden and Nanking, the recognition

of the sovereignty over China of Chungking alone, and finally an agreement between Japan and America whereby Japan covertly abrogated the casus foederis as defined by the Tripartite Pact.

Were the American President and his Secretary of State so far from a true appreciation of the situation as to think that their ten articles of November 26 could really lead to a revival of peaceful intentions on the part of the Japanese? It is hardly credible, there being clear evidence that Japanese diplomatic correspondence was an open book to them. It cannot have escaped their notice that as the days passed and his anxieties grew, Togo notified his embassy in Washington that beyond a certain date limit, finally fixed for November 29, relations between Japan and America, in view of the inability to find a compromise, "would disintegrate in chaos",

Mitsubishi A6M Zero-Sen 'Zeke' takes off from aircraft carrier.

or that "events would occur of their own accord."

Preparations for war

However, on November 25, the day before the American counter-proposals for a modus vivendi were handed to the Japanese envoys, the Defense Committee, presided over by President Roosevelt, and attended by the Secretaries of State, of War, and of the Navy, the Chief of the General Staff and the Chief of Naval Operations, held its weekly meeting. Afterwards, Harry Stimson, the Secretary of War, made this entry in his diary: "How could the Japanese be got into a situation where they would have to fire the first shot, and without leaving ourselves too exposed?

That was the question."

And that is not all, because, on November 27, Knox, Secretary of the Navy, in a communication to his department heads, wrote:

"This dispatch is to be considered a war warning. Negotiations with Japan looking toward stabilization of conditions in the Pacific have ceased and an aggressive move by Japan is expected within the next few days."

Certainly, at the time that he sent out this warning, Knox might have been in possession of the decoded despatch which Kurusu and Nomura had sent to Togo the previous day, at the conclusion of which they made known the degree of amazement they felt at the Secretary of State's latest proposals. But it was not till the day following the warning reproduced above that the Japanese Minister of Foreign Affairs announced the imminent rupture of negotiations.

From the texts quoted above it appears that the American administration applied the "semi-positive" method in its relations with Japan, forcing on Japan responsibility for the last word which, in the view of President Roosevelt's entourage, would be war. And certainly in Washington this contingency was contemplated with complete optimism. Stimson, the Secretary of War, indeed wrote on October 21: "An extraordinarily favourable strategic situation has just developed in the South-West Pacific. All the strategic options open to us during the last 20 years have been totally transformed in the last six months. Whereas we were unable before to change the course of events, suddenly we find ourselves possessed of enormous potential, whose full possibilities we are as yet unable to appreciate."

Pearl Harbor orders go out

At all events, the ten articles of the modus vivendi proposed to Japan by the State Department played into the hands of General Tojo and those of his cabinet who were urging war against the United States, Great Britain, and the Netherlands. On November 29 an "Imperial Conference" assembled, consisting of ministers in office and the leading Japanese politicians of the past few years. The fateful decision was approved by a majority on a count of everyone present; Emperor Hirohito gave tacit consent, and on December 2 somewhere between the Kurile Islands and Hawaii, Admiral Nagumo, commanding the Air Attack and Support Forces, received the message agreed upon: "Climb Mount Niitaka", signifying the order to attack the fleet anchored at Pearl Harbor at dawn on Sunday, December 7, 1941.

Prince Fumimaro Konoye, born in 1891, became Prime Minister of Japan in June 1937. A somewhat tragic figure, he failed to prevent the Chinese war or to bring it to a speedy end; he failed to restrain the extreme militarists; and he failed to reach agreement with the United States. Konoye was the main hope of all Japanese moderates but he was never able to prevail over War Minister Tojo, and resigned two months before the attack on Pearl Harbor. His successor was Tojo. He held office after the war, but killed himself when about to be tried as a war criminal.

Did the U.S. know?

Quite apart from the strictly military enquiries, the "mystery of Pearl Harbor" or, perhaps better, the mystery of the surprise at Pearl Harbor, has been the subject of a congressional enquiry in Washington whose proceedings, published in 1946, fill 40 volumes.

In regard to the controversy produced by Rear-Admiral R. A. Theobald's book, referred to above, use has been made of Volume III of the History of United States Naval Operations in World War II, whose author, Professor Samuel Eliot Morison, of Harvard University, enlisted in the United States Navy in 1942 as a historiographer with the rank of Lieutenant-Commander. In spite of its official character, it is a work which is totally objective and can be recommended both on account of the abundance and the reliability of its information.

More recently, in 1962, Mrs. Roberta Wohlstetter published a large volume at the University of Stanford, California, devoted to the same question. Pearl Harbor is a masterpiece of critical analysis, every significant document is examined, and the conclusions drawn are quite unbiased. The author is fully conversant with the different questions relating to the political and military information services, how they functioned, the constraints imposed upon them, and the extent and limit of their possibilities.

The question that is most pertinent could be put briefly as follows: bearing in mind that Colonel William S. Friedmann and his team of cipher experts in Washington had managed to "break" the Japanese diplomatic codes within the required time, how did it come about that the Pacific Fleet at Pearl Harbor did not receive warning of the stratagem that was being prepared to take them by surprise there where they lay at anchor?

Was Roosevelt to blame?

To this, Rear-Admiral R. A. Theobald's reply is: because President Roosevelt and his advisers (principally, General Marshall and Admiral Stark) had made up their minds that the fleet should play the part of the goat that is left tethered to the post as bait for the Japanese tiger, and that the risk to which it was thereby exposed was the one means of provoking the attack which would bring the United States irrevocably into the war.

It is perfectly true that none of the five electronic machines built to decipher the "Purple Code" of the Japanese was allocated to Pearl Harbor, nor was Rear-Admiral Kimmel among those who received the "Magic" messages which recorded the transcription of Japanese secret despatches. But, it is common knowledge that the secrecy surrounding the activity of decoding services is, in every country in the world, the most jealously guarded of all; increasing the circulation of "Magic" messages would have involved a serious risk of disclosure, which was at all costs to be avoided, and it is a fact that in July and August 1945, the "purple machine" was still unscrambling radio correspondence between the Japanese Ministry of Foreign Affairs and its representatives in Moscow, Stockholm, and Berne.

Besides, Togo's despatches contained nothing relating to Pearl Harbor for the excellent reason that he had no knowledge whatsoever of the operation en trusted to Admiral Nagumo. On the other hand, it would have been of use to Kimmel to know that, after the end of September, the Japanese consul in Honolulu received the order to communicate the exact moorings of all major American warships.

But this clue, which seems so obvious to us today, was just one among a host of others which singled out Malaya and the Dutch colonies as the single objective of Japanese aggression, and with such conclusiveness that some sources in Washington even forecast that the Philippines would be spared.

On the afternoon of December 6, the Navy's "purple machine" decoded Togo's final instructions to his envoys in Washington. They were followed by a message containing 13 points to be completed by a fourteenth on the following morning. The complete document was to be handed to the Secretary of State at 1300 hours on December 7; when it was shown to President Roosevelt, it drew from him the exclamation: "This is war!" And, in fact, the thirteenth paragraph included the statement:

"The (American) Proposal menaces the Empire's existence itself and disparages its honor and prestige. Therefore, viewed in its entirety, the Japanese Government regrets that it cannot accept the proposal as a basis for negotiation."

Yet nothing was done to alert the Pacific Fleet of the imminence of hostilities. But if Rear-Admiral R. A. Theobald interprets this silence as supporting his thesis, it can be advanced against him that the fleet had already, on November 27, been placed on the alert by the Chief of Naval Operations.

The attack is planned

And this brings us to Pearl Harbor itself. There, on the previous March 31, a report drawn up by two senior officers, one Army, one Navy, drew attention to the danger to which the base was exposed from a carrier-borne aircraft attack. But this prediction was disregarded, Japanese naval concentration seeming to converge on points in South-East Asia. And this thesis appeared to receive confirmation in the "ultimatum" of November 27, according to which Siam, the Kra isthmus (the narrowest part of the Malay peninsula), North Borneo, and the Philippines seemed to be the particular points of possible attack. And, doubtless, it was thought that the huge Japanese aircraft-carriers, which had been out of radio contact for several weeks past, were to cover an amphibious campaign.

Within the Pacific Fleet, to have maintained a permanent state of readiness would have impaired the action training programme, and on that point Admiral Kimmel was not prepared to compromise, because the operational order Rainbow 5 that it was his task to execute required him to lead his forces to attack the Marshall, then the Caroline, Islands.

In the Army Air Force, Major-General W. Short, commanding the military district of Hawaii had, on sight of the "ultimatum", been concerned above all to prevent acts of sabotage which were to be expected on the part of enemy agents introduced into the archipelago's large Japanese colony, and this led him to order his planes to be close-packed on airfields, rather than dispersed. Furthermore, reconnaissance patrols round Oahu Island suffered from the fact that the intensive training programme for fighters and bombers had left insufficient stocks of fuel for reconnaissance.

Finally, liaison between the naval and air force information services was insufficient and unreliable, while within the Pacific Fleet and the military district of Hawaii, radio communications left a lot to be desired.

But rather than adopt Rear-Admiral Theobald's argument concerning Washington's responsibilities in the Pearl Harbor disaster, one is inclined to give credence rather to Professor Morison. He points out that the commanders of the U.S. armed forces may have fallen into a very simple but dangerous trap: that of considering what they thought the enemy was likely to do and formulating contingency plans based upon that, rather than assessing all the possibilities open to the enemy and being prepared for any eventuality. Though often pointed out, this is an error all too simple to fall into.

Seen in this light, the surprise attack on December 7, 1941 is the exact replica of that in the Ardennes on May 10, 1940. It follows, however, that Morison's judgement embraces Admiral Stark and General Marshall in Washington as well as Kimmel and Short in Honolulu.

Pearl Harbor's fate was set.

USS Arizona in flames after being attacked by Japanese fighter-bombers.

It was early in January 1941 that Admiral Yamamoto, commanding the Combined Fleet, instructed a small group of staff officers to make a study of a surprise attack on Pearl Harbor, which would be made by carrier-borne aircraft. Until then, the Japanese Admiralty had contemplated adopting a defensive posture towards the American Pacific forces. But it became apparent that only a single devastating blow dealt at the enemy's principal naval formation at the beginning of hostilities would guarantee Japan the smooth conquest of her objectives in South-East Asia. Was the idea for such an enterprise suggested to her by the remarkable success of the Fleet Air Arm's attack on Taranto on November 11 of the previous year? It seems highly probable, in view of the fact that at the end of May 1941, a mission from the Japanese Naval Air Force visited Taranto and was given a detailed account of the course of events in Operation "Judgement".

In the following August, a series of strategic map exercises carried out under the supervision of Admiral Yamamoto provided the basis for Operational Order No. 1, which was signed on November 1. In the meantime, he had converted his colleagues to his plan, some of them having at first found it too risky, others objecting that the expeditionary corps destined for South-East Asia was being excessively weakened; but further and most important, Yamamoto had made his aircrews undergo a period of intensive training.

Under the orders of Vice-Admiral Chuichi Nagumo, the task force given the mission of attacking Pearl Harbor included six aircraft carriers (Kaga, Akagi, Hiryu, Soryu, Zuikaku, and Shokaku) with a total complement of 432 planes; two fast

Battleship Row after attack.

battleships (Hiei and Kirishima); three cruisers (two heavy and one light); nine destroyers; three submarines, which were to patrol the itinerary plotted; and eight tankers to refuel the squadron at sea.

In the eventuality of Japan's deciding on war, the attack would take place at dawn on December 7, a Sunday, when the American fleet was normally at its moorings. In the words of Rear-Admiral Matome Ugaki, chief-of-staff of the task force, addressing his unit commanders, the attack on Pearl Harbor would be the Waterloo of the war that was to follow. Furthermore, the damage from the air attacks would be added to by those delivered by midget submarines carried to Oahu by ocean-going submarines.

Heard at Pearl Harbor:

"All hands, general quarters! Air raid! This is no drill!"

"Padre, there's planes out there and they look like Japs."

"Hell, I didn't even know they were sore at us."

"We're not giving up this ship yet!"

"To hell with fuse settings-shoot!"

"TORA-TORA-TORA!"

On November 22, the 31 units commanded by Vice-Admiral Nagumo assembled in a deserted bay on the island of Etorofu, the southernmost of the Kurile chain. On the 26th, the Japanese task force set sail, but, as has been said, the order to attack was to be communicated in a coded message and this came on December 2. The course charted ran east along the 43rd Parallel, thus, with the fog that prevails in those Pacific latitudes, rendering any accidental encounter with other ships unlikely.

On December 6, after nightfall, the formation set course for its objective. The news that no aircraft-carrier was present in Pearl Harbor caused some disappointment among the Japanese pilots. On the other hand, listening to the light-hearted radio programmes coming from Hawaii, it seemed quite clear that the Americans suspected nothing.

Nagumo launches his first strike

The following day, Sunday December 7, at 0615, Nagumo, who was by then 230 miles from Pearl Harbor, despatched a first wave of 214 machines, including 50 conventional bombers, 51 dive-bombers and 70 torpedo planes. One hour later, this formation appeared on a training radar screen, at a range of approximately 160 miles. But this information, which would have given 30 minutes warning to the Pacific Fleet, was not reported by the young air force officer to whom it had been passed because of the coincidence that a formation of Flying Fortresses coming from California was expected at the same time and from the same direction.

Lieutenant-Commander Nakaya, who was leading the fighters in the first wave, saw Pearl Harbor at about 0750:

"Pearl Harbor was still asleep in the morning mist. It was calm and serene inside the harbor, not even a trace of smoke from the ships at Oahu. The orderly group of barracks, the wriggling white line of the automobile road climbing up to the mountain-top; fine objectives of attack in all directions. In line with these, inside the harbor, were important ships of the Pacific Fleet, strung out and anchored two ships side by side in an orderly manner."

A few minutes later, two radio messages crossed: at 0753, Captain Fuchida signalled Akagi: "Surprise successful"; at 0758, Rear-Admiral Patrick Bellinger from his H.Q. on Ford Island sent out in plain language: "Air raid, Pearl Harbor — this is no drill."

First objective: seven battleships

Of the 127 ships under the command of Rear-Admiral Husband E. Kimmel, 94 were at berth and preparing for the ceremony of the colours. But the Japanese concentrated their efforts on the seven battleships moored in pairs alongside Ford Island, which stands in the middle of the roadstead. One 1,760-

Battleships after attack, from left. USS West Virginia, USS Tennesse, USS Arizona.

pound bomb blew up the forward magazine of Arizona, while another dropped down the funnel and exploded in the engine room. The ship settled quickly and went down with Rear-Admiral Isaac C. Kidd and 1,106 officers, petty officers, and other ranks out of a crew of 1,511. Struck by three torpedoes, Oklahoma capsized almost instantaneously, trapping below decks 415 men, some of whom survived until Christmas Eve. Had it not been for the extraordinary presence of mind of their crews in taking action to right the two ships, West Virginia and California would have met the same fate; Nevada was hit by a torpedo and

two bombs but shot down three of her attackers. Maryland and Tennessee escaped relatively lightly and were able, after December 20, to leave Oahu for an American dockyard, together with Pennsylvania, which had been in dry-dock, and thus out of reach of torpedoes. Three cruisers and three destroyers also suffered damage.

The Japanese pilot Nuzo Mori gives the following account of his feelings as he flew his torpedo plane in to attack an American battleship:

"I manoeuvred in order to make my line of approach absolutely right, knowing that the depth of water in the harbour was rarely more than 35 feet. The slightest error in speed or

Wreckage USS Cassin & Downess.

altitude when firing might upset the mechanism of the torpedo and make it go to the bottom or break surface, undoing all my efforts either way.

"At the time, I was hardly aware of my actions. I acted like an automaton through force of habit which my long training had given me.

"The battleship appeared to leap suddenly into view across the front of my machine, looming huge like a vast grey mountain.

"Stand by! ... Fire! ...

"All the while, I completely forgot the enemy fire and the throbbing of my own engine, totally absorbed by my manoeuvre. At the right moment, I pulled with all my strength on the release lever. The machine jolted violently as shells hit the wings and fuselage. My head was flung back, and I felt as though I'd just hit an iron bar headon. But I'd made it! The torpedo-launching was perfect! My plane still flew and responded to my control. The torpedo was going to score a direct hit. I suddenly became conscious of where I was and of the intensity of the enemy fire."

The second wave attacks

At 0715, Nagumo launched his second strike, consisting of 54 bombers, 80 dive-bombers, and 36 fighters. Led by Lieutenant-Commander Shimazaki, it completed the work of the first wave in the harbour, then turned its attention to the naval installations on Ford Island,

Wheeler and Hickham Fields (the air force bases), and the flying boat station at Kaneohe, destroying 65 aircraft out of the 231 on Oahu. In men, American losses for the day totalled 2,403 killed and 1,178 wounded.

Japan's losses: a mere fleabite

This tremendous success cost Nagumo 29 planes and 55 airmen. After recovering the aircraft of the second strike, Nagumo set course north at 1300. The midget submarine attack was a complete failure, however, and on December 10 one of the transport submarines was sent to the bottom by an aircraft from the carrier Enterprise. Moreover, the Japanese omitted to attack the vast oil storage tanks at Pearl Harbor, whose destruction would have incapacitated the U.S. fleet for months. American soldiers and sailors had acted so swiftly to re-establish the situation that Nagumo abandoned a third assault, as he thought that its cost in aircraft would be prohibitive — conclusive enough proof that Kimmel had shown energy and intelligence in training his crews.

Yamamoto — if one may be forgiven an analogy from boxing — had flattered himself that he would knock out the U.S. Navy in the first round; in fact, he had merely left it groggy but upright. The destruction of two battleships and the damage sustained by six others did not deprive it of its main striking force: its three

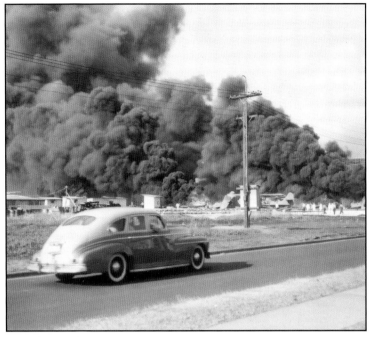

Kaneohe Naval Air Station.

aircraft-carriers were intact and with them 20 cruisers and 65 destroyers. Above all, the attack on December 7 mobilised all American resources and raised a mighty wave of indignation across the United States which with steadily mounting strength would break on Japan with colossal force.

Vengeance is sworn

"A date which will live in infamy," said Roosevelt, giving an account of the events before Congress. And, on the bridge of Enterprise as she headed back to Pearl Harbor on December 9, Rear-Admiral William F. Halsey echoed him when, at the sight of the wrecks obstructing the fairway at Ford Island he made this, less academic, utterance: "Before we're through with 'em, the Japanese language will be spoken only in hell!"

Declaration of War - President Franklin D Roosewlt delivers message of war to Congress.

HMS Prince of Wales Royal Navy.

In the spring of 1939, with the threat of war in Europe posed by Germany and Italy, the case of Japanese intervention on the side of the Axis powers was examined in the course of conversations between the British and French staff officers who drew up the Allied war plans. If Japan joined in the war, the French Navy was to assume responsibility for operations throughout the Mediterranean while the British naval forces based on Alexandria sailed to reinforce those at Singapore.

The armistice signed at Rethondes on June 22, 1940 caused reverberations as far as the Far East, because it was now out of the question for the British Mediterranean Fleet to abandon the Mediterranean to the Italian Navy. Thus the naval defence of South-East Asia against the emergent threat by Japan was reduced to an absolute minimum, even allowing for the small Dutch force based on the East Indies, which effectively took its orders from the British War Cabinet. Graver still, while in 1939 the British could still consider French Indo-China as the bastion of Malaya, two years later, the agreements forced on Vichy by Tokyo turned Saigon into a Japanese pistol aimed at Singapore; and already Japanese technical missions were finding their way into Siam.

It is clear that, faced with the defence of the Far East, on which in the last analysis depended that of Australia and New Zealand, the Imperial General Staff and the War Cabinet found themselves with an extremely difficult problem, in spite of the fact that Roosevelt, at the Atlantic Conference, had given Churchill his guarantee that he would consider any new Japanese violation of territory in this global sector as a ground for war and that he would inform the Tokyo Government accordingly.

Japanese aircraft sink Repulse and Prince of Wales

Before dawn on December 10, Rear-Admiral Matsunaga despatched 11 reconnaissance planes, 52 torpedo planes, and 34 level bombers, belonging to his 22nd Air Flotilla, from Saigon.

General Douglas MacArthur, Supreme Commander of the United States Forces in Australia and the South-West Pacific and Allied Supreme Commander in the Pacific at the end of the war, was born in 1880. He served with the American Expeditionary Force in France at the end of World War I. In 1941 MacArthur was military adviser to the Philippine Government, but was recalled to active service with the U.S. Army in July. He was appointed commander of the U.S. land forces in the Far East, which also included the Philippine Army. He conducted the defence of the area until pulled out by President Roosevelt to take command of the U.S. forces in Australia in March 1942. MacArthur decided that the defence of Australia hinged on that of New Guinea, and so made Port Moresby his main base. Here he slowly built up his forces and developed the strategy of cutting off large Japanese forces and then leaving them to rot, rather than attacking them head on and destroying them, suffering heavy losses himself in the process. With these tactics MacArthur was able to start pushing back towards the Philippines in 1943. The Philippines were reached in late 1944 and largely overrun in 1945.

The surrender of Japan was accepted by MacArthur on September 2, 1945.

At the same instant, the two British capital ships, escorted by three destroyers, were on course for Kuantan. Phillips had abandoned his plan to attack the Japanese landing force at Singora when his chief-of-staff had informed him that fighter cover was impossible, and decided to return to Singapore. En route he had been informed of possible enemy landings at Kuantan and concluded that he should investigate. Having ascertained that all was normal and that nothing untoward was happening, Sir Tom Phillips headed back for Singapore. At about 1100 hours, when he had Kuantan on his beam, the first enemy planes appeared in the sky. The fire from the British ships was as poor as the aim of the Japanese bombers, who managed to get only three out of 57 bombs on target; but the torpedo planes attacked with consummate skill, setting up a crossfire of torpedoes to defeat any attempt at avoiding action on the part of Repulse and Prince of Wales. The former sank half an hour after noon, the latter less than an hour later.

What can be more tragic for a commanding officer than to witness his ship's agony? The following account by a British naval officer vividly conveys the intense personal drama of Repulse's captain, W. G. Tennant, after he had given the order to abandon ship:

"As she heeled rapidly over, Captain Tennant clambered over the side of the bridge on to what had previously been a vertical surface and was walking unsteadily along it when the sea seemed to come up and engulf him. The ship must have rolled right over on top of him, for everything at once became pitch dark, telling him he was a long way down under water. The defeatist part of the mind that we all possess whispered to him that this was the end of things and that he might as well take in water and get it over. But another part of his brain bade him react against this advice, and he decided to hang on to life as long as possible; though he wondered if he could possibly hold his breath long enough to come up again. Lumps of wood hit him in the darkness. After what seemed a long, long time the water began to show a faint lightening, and suddenly he was on the surface in swirling water, luckily close to a Carley float, the occupants of which hauled him on board still wearing his steel helmet. The destroyers Vampire and Electra were coming up to pick up survivors and soon had them on board."

Of the 2,921 officers and other ranks who manned the two capital ships, 2,081 were picked up by the destroyers who went to their rescue with no concern for the risk to themselves; Admiral Sir Tom Phillips, however, went down with Prince of Wales as did her commanding officer, Captain J. C. Leach who, on May 24 of the same year, had been one of two survivors out of the 11 men on the bridge of his vessel when it was struck by a shell from Bismarck. Just as rescue operations were being completed, nine R.A.F. fighter planes from the Singapore base appeared in the sky. In enumerating the causes of this disaster, unprecedented in the annals of the Royal Navy, Captain Russell Grenfell indicts principally:

"The presence in London of a Minister of Defence so convinced of his own individual competence as a master of naval strategy that he was prepared to ignore the advice of his professional naval experts and force upon them measures for the naval defence of Malaya which they clearly did not like."

And one is left no choice but to confirm this opinion. As for the initiative taken by the ill-fated Sir Tom Phillips, it was that to be expected of a British sailor, bred in the tradition of taking the offensive and promoted to his high command by virtue of this very fighting spirit.

American submarines powerless

The loss of Prince of Wales and of Repulse was a considerable relief to the 2nd and 3rd Japanese Fleets which, under the command of Vice-Admirals Kondo and Takahashi, had the task of protecting, then supplying the 14th and 25th Armies, which would go on to conquer respectively the Philippines and the Malayan peninsula, including Singapore.

If the American, Dutch, and British cruisers and destroyers in this theatre of operations on December 10, 1941 were ineffective, being old and open to attack from the air, the 42 submarines under the orders of Admirals Helfrich at Surabaja and Thomas Hart at Manila did not perform much better; certainly, the Dutch registered some successes, but the Americans had the bitter experience of finding that their magnetic detonators worked no better than those carried by U-boats in 1940; this extract from a series of reports collected by Captain Edward L. Beach provides evidence of this:

"Fired three torpedoes, bubble tracks of two could plainly be seen through the periscope, tracked by sight and sound

Japanese troops come ashore.

right through target. They looked like sure hits from here. No explosions. Cannot understand it."

In such advantageous conditions, it is hardly surprising that the amphibious operation set in motion by the Japanese High Command on December 8 proceeded as planned.

In the Philippines, General Douglas MacArthur disposed of rather more than 31,000 men (19,000 Americans) against General Homma's 14th Army, which began the assault with two divisions. It was the same story in the air, the attacking force having 750 planes, the defence 300, at the moment, that is, when Clark Field was bombed, involving a loss of 17 out of 36 Flying Fortresses and several fighters destroyed on the ground. The lack of spare

runways has been put forward as explaining the success of this operation, carried out only a few hours after Manila had received the news of Pearl Harbor.

Japan's flood-tide of conquest

On December 10, 1941, General Homma established a first beach-head at Aparri in the north of Luzon, with the intention of engaging the defence at this spot while effecting a second landing in the bay of Lingayen in order to outflank and destroy it. But MacArthur was too quick for him. At the first sign of the enemy's second manoeuvre, he disengaged, but far from trying to block the Japanese advance on Manila, he side-stepped, so to speak, placing his troops across the peninsula of Bataan, which shuts off the bay of Cavite, in positions prepared beforehand. When, on December 27, Homma got over his surprise, the Americans and Filipinos were so well dug in that it took the Japanese five months to drive them out of their last stronghold. Hong Kong was the objective of General Sakai's 23rd Army. The defence of the island city of Victoria and Kowloon on the mainland devolved upon Major-General C. M. Maltby with 12,000 men, a force which was hardly to be adequate for the task.

On the night of December 9–10 the Japanese stormed the defence of Kowloon peninsula and forced the British troops to fall back on to the island after three days' severe fighting. On the 18th, again under cover of darkness, the Japanese 38th Division crossed the strait separating Victoria from the continent. In spite of vastly superior enemy forces, Major-General Maltby continued to resist until shortage of ammunition obliged him to accede to the third call to surrender. The cease-fire came on Christmas Day 1941.

On the day that the first Japanese landings took place at Singora, Air Chief-Marshal Sir Robert Brooke-Popham was C.-in-C. of combined British forces in the Far East. The planes at his disposal were woefully inadequate, as has already been observed. If the state of his troops, under the command of General Percival, was somewhat better, it was still far from satisfactory: no tanks, little artillery, and the infantry a mixture of British, Indian, Australian and Malay. In training and tactics Percival's forces could not compete with the enemy. Neither had the troops been positioned in the most effective manner.

The Japanese 25th Army's mission was to fly the Rising Sun over Singapore on DDay plus 100, counting from the first landing, that is to say March 16, 1942. With three, subsequently four divisions (27, then 36 battalions), its numerical superiority over the British was only slight. The Japanese forces, however, were crack formations and had the initial advantage of surprise. Furthermore, their abundant aircraft support would thwart British attempts to reform and regain the initiative. To this end, the numerous airfields in the Malay peninsula which the R.A.F. had put into service proved invaluable. And the army had at its head an outstandingly dynamic and resourceful leader in General Yamashita — "Rommel of the jungle" as he was known. (Yamashita had a reputation for cruelty, but in other respects the resemblance was fully de served.) Advancing by means of constant infiltration and outflanking movements, he forced Percival to abandon position after position, never leaving him time to entrench himself; many times, in order to further his objective, he "mixed" (his own description) his own commandos in with retreating British troops with the aim of preventing a "scorched earth" policy being carried out.

By the end of the year General Yamashita was ahead of schedule. The fall of Kota Bharu provided him with an excellent base for air attacks on Singapore, as well as an easy path to the Indian Ocean. Once there, he commandeered everything that would float, and, with a barrage of tiny amphibious operations prodding at the British rear areas, unnerved the British completely.

In Siam, General Iida, commanding the 15th Army, found every door opened for him by a collaborator government. By the

British gun carriers in jungle.

end of December, after what may be described as a "route march", he reached the frontier with Burma to whose defence Lieutenant-General T. J. Hutton had just been appointed. The means at hand to do so were exiguous to say the least, and will be covered in a later chapter.

With the exception of Guam, the Mariana group of islands was transferred from Germany to become a Japanese mandate by the Treaty of Versailles in 1919. Hence the American island of Guam was left virtually indefensible and surrendered on December 10.

It remained for Wake Island, half way between Guam and Midway, to inflict a first reverse on the Japanese, whose offensive in other sectors was so successful and auspicious. An exceptionally

timely reinforcement had arrived on December 4 in the shape of a squadron of Grumman F4F "Wildcat" fighter-bombers, and the atoll's garrison repelled a first assault, even managing to sink two Japanese destroyers. Exasperated by this humiliating setback, Yamamoto ordered Nagumo to detach the carriers Hiryu and Soryu, two cruisers, and two destroyers so as to contrive a fresh assault.

On December 21, the last Wildcat was shot down, but not before it had itself disposed of two Zero fighters. Then the dive bombers destroyed the batteries defending the island, reducing them one by one. On December 23, overwhelmed by the Japanese landings, the heroic garrison at Wake at last surrendered.

Burmese railway bridge blown-up by retreating British and Indian troops, guarded by a Japanese sentry.

On September 11, 1941, General Marshall and Admiral Stark sketched out to President Roosevelt the "main lines of the military policy" which they thought should be adopted, and proposed that these should be implemented without delay. In this extensive document they drew the President's attention to the enormous danger that the Third Reich would be to America if it were given the time to reorganise the continent of Europe as it liked. They therefore both agreed:

"The principal strategic method employed by the United States in the immediate future should be the material support of present military operations against Germany, and their reinforcement by active participation in the war by the United States while holding Japan in check pending future developments."

For this purpose, the "maintenance of an active front in Russia" appeared extremely important to them, and it was also imperative to "prevent Axis penetration into North Africa and the islands of the Atlantic" (Cape Verdes, Canaries, Madeira, and Azores).

These proposals, which were accepted by the President, also met the wishes of the British cabinet. In effect, Hitler and Mussolini, by declaring war on the United States, had saved Roosevelt the difficulty of persuading Congress that the best way to avenge Pearl Harbor would be to have two more new enemies on America's hands. Nevertheless, just when Churchill was preparing to put the case for Operation "Gymnast" (an American landing in Algeria in conjunction with an 8th Army drive into Tunisia) to the men responsible for American strategy, it was already apparent to the latter that their forces were unable to keep Japan at bay anywhere in the Far East.

But this order of priorities, in which the defeat of Germany would take priority over that of Japan, was not questioned by Roosevelt, Marshall, and Stark at the "Arcadia" Conference in Washington at the end of 1941. On the contrary, Marshall and Stark (the latter of whom was later replaced by Admiral Ernest J. King) took up an unequivocal position on the matter from the time of their first meeting with their British colleagues:

"… notwithstanding the entry of Japan into the war, our view remains that Germany is still the prime enemy and her defeat is the key to victory. Once Germany is defeated the collapse of Italy and the defeat of Japan must follow."

Agreement was reached on the principle of such a landing on January 12, whereupon the plan was reworked as "SuperGymnast". According to this new version, three British and three American divisions were to land in Morocco and Algeria from April 15 onwards. At the same time, three more American divisions would cross the Atlantic and relieve three British divisions in Northern Ireland. The latter

It was maintained among General Douglas MacArthur's staff that this decision had been wrung from Roosevelt by Churchill's plausible eloquence. This was not in fact so; the American Chiefs-of-Staff, quite independently of the British and for purely national reasons, were already entirely in favour of the

"Germany first" principle. However, it must be noted that in his memoirs MacArthur, the defender of the Philippines, claims that he was kept in ignorance of this important decision, and it is understandable that as a result of this omission he remained somewhat bitter against Marshall.

On the other hand, no great importance need be attached to the criticism MacArthur made of Admiral King, the new Chief of Naval Operations, when he wrote:

"Although Admiral King felt that the fleet did not have sufficient resources to proceed to Manila, it was my impression that our Navy depreciated its own strength and might well have cut through to relieve our hard-pressed forces. The Japanese blockade of the Philippines was to some extent a paper blockade. Mindanao was still accessible and firmly held by us. The bulk of the Japanese Navy, operating on tight schedules, was headed south for the seizure of Borneo, Malaya and Indonesia. American carriers having escaped destruction at Pearl Harbor could have approached the Philippines and unloaded planes on fields in Mindanao."

Writing about Pearl Harbor shortly before his death in 1966, Admiral Chester W. Nimitz, who must share with MacArthur the credit for the final defeat of Japan, said:

"No one regrets more than I our 3,000 dead when the Japanese attacked Pearl Harbor. But if Admiral Husband Kimmel, who at that time commanded the American forces at Pearl Harbor, had had information of the attack 24 hours in advance, he would have sent off all our forces to meet the Japanese.

"We had not one aircraft-carrier capable of opposing Admiral

Nagumo's aircraft-carrier formation, and the Japanese would have sunk all our ships on the high seas.

"We would have lost 6,000 men and almost all our Pacific Fleet."

This was the position on the day of the attack. But on the next day, when the aircraft-carriers Lexington and Enterprise reached Pearl Harbor, there was no question of sending them out on an operation against six other carriers without the advantage of surprise. Moreover, the six aircraft-carriers of the Japanese striking force each carried at least 60 planes, all superior in performance to the 80 machines on each of the American carriers.

MacArthur's proposed operation would therefore in all probability have led to a second Pearl Harbor, but this time in mid-ocean, with no hope of rescue.

Malaya in danger

The Japanese offensive, making full use of its considerable matériel superiority, particularly at sea and in the air, was now in full spate, with its right wing threatening Burma and its left Australia. Success followed success.

Lieutenant-General A. E. Percival, G.O.C. Malaya, had III Indian Corps with which to try to oppose the Japanese advance. This corps, under the command of Lieutenant-General Sir Lewis Heath, disposed of three divisions, the 9th and 11th Indian in the line and the 8th Australian in reserve. Percival, faced with the problem of defending the Malay Peninsula, at places 175 miles wide, was forced to deploy his forces to cover the main axial roads, while the Japanese either infiltrated the British line through the jungle or bypassed the British positions by carrying out amphibious landings in their rear.

British weaknesses

Although the British forces enjoyed a slight superiority in numbers over their opponents (88,000 allied troops to 70,000 Japanese), their formations were inferior in training. The crack Japanese divisions were more than a match for those troops facing them. The British, moreover, had deployed well forward in northern Malaya to cover airfields for which, in the event, no air cover could be found. To reinforce these stretched dispositions, it is true that convoys were bringing in considerable reinforcements: an Indian brigade on January 3, the 53rd Brigade of the 18th Division from Britain on the 13th, a second Indian brigade on the 22nd, and the rest of the 18th Division on the 29th. But the training of the Indian troops was entirely inadequate, and the British division, which had originally been intended for the Middle East and diverted to Malaya at the Cape of Good Hope, had declined in efficiency during its long sea passage.

The new Japanese objectives

Meanwhile, the Japanese Navy had also been moving forward, stretching out its tentacles to seize the bases it coveted, as Admiral Morison puts it. These tentacles consisted of the 2nd Scouting Fleet, 3rd Blockade and Transport Fleet, and 4th Mandate Fleet. The 2nd Scouting Fleet, commanded by Vice-Admiral Kondo, was to assist in the capture of Malaya and the reduction of the "impregnable" fortress of Singapore; the 3rd Blockade and

Transport Fleet, under Vice-Admiral Takahashi, was ordered to gain possession of the Philippines, Borneo, and Celebes and then to join forces with the 2nd Scouting Fleet in order to take the Dutch East Indies, with their coveted oilfields; and the 4th Mandate Fleet, commanded by Vice-Admiral Inouye, was to take Guam and Wake. The attainment of these objectives would secure the perimeter of the Greater South-East Asia Co-Prosperity Sphere.

It should also be noted here that the Japanese land-based airforces co-operated very efficiently with the 2nd and 3rd Fleets, which had no carriers. From December 15, 1941 they operated from the base at Davao on the island of Mindanao; Kendari airfield, in the south of Celebes, was captured in record time on January 17 and was soon in full swing as a Japanese advanced base; Amboina, in the Moluccas, was captured on February 3. From these bases, the Japanese could wreak havoc over the whole area of operations assigned to the 2nd and 3rd Fleets.

Besides being better trained than the Allied pilots opposing them, the Japanese had a distinct advantage in numbers and matériel. Most of the Hawker Hurricanes which had reached Singapore on January 14 were quickly overwhelmed in the air or destroyed on the ground, and a second consignment of these fighters, the only Allied aircraft in the theatre capable of taking on the Zero at anything like even terms, was diverted to Java. And thus the Japanese bombers had a field day at little cost. On February 3, Surabaja in Java was bombed for the first time; the next day the American cruisers Houston and Marblehead were both hit, the second badly enough to have to return to Australia for repairs.

Borneo and Sumatra invaded

The first Japanese landing on Borneo occurred at Miri, on December 16. The oil port of Tarakan, near the entrance to the Makassar Strait, and Manado, at the northern tip of Celebes, both fell on the same day, January 11, 1942. During the night of January 24, a division of American destroyers surprised the Japanese as they were landing an invasion force at Balikpapan, where most of Borneo's oil was refined, and sank four merchantmen, but this success could not alter the course of events. Without even taking into account the fall of Kendari and Amboina, or waiting for the capture of Singapore, the Japanese invaded Sumatra, on February 14, and Timor on the 20th, without making any distinction between the Portuguese and Dutch parts of the island. This advance was of great strategic import, as it breached the "Malay barrier" and thus gave the Japanese the opportunity of cutting communications with Australia.

The situation was now beyond any hope of remedy, and on February 25 Wavell received orders to move his headquarters back to Ceylon, to which he had been preceded, on February 14, by Admiral Hart. Command of the Allied naval forces still operating against the Japanese had devolved upon the Dutch Vice-Admiral C. E. L. Helfrich, who was later to show exceptional courage in a disastrous situation.

Battle of the Java Sea

Meanwhile, the Allied advanced head quarters at Bandung in Java had received information that two convoys, totalling 97 transports and with powerful escorts, had been observed off the Malay Peninsula and leaving the Makassar Strait. These were in fact the convoys carrying the Japanese 16th Army to the invasion of Java. With three divisions and one brigade, this force was far superior to the 30,000 trained troops with which General ter Poorten had to conduct the defence of Java.

Java's only hope lay in the destruction of the two convoys before they reached the island. To this end, the Allied naval forces in the area were dispatched under the Dutch Rear-Admiral Karel Doorman to the decisive Battle of the Java Sea. The Allied force, however, was at a distinct disadvantage as it had not had the time to learn to co-ordinate its efforts properly and to work out a common signalling code. Doorman's command consisted of two heavy cruisers, the British Exeter and American Houston; three light cruisers, the Dutch De Ruyter and Java, and the Australian Perth; and nine destroyers, four American, three British, and two Dutch.

On February 27, at 1500, Doorman was at sea off Surabaja when he received orders to intercept the Japanese convoy heading from the Makassar Strait towards Surabaja. Contact was made at about 1615 between the Allied force and the Japanese escort under Rear-Admiral Nishimura: the heavy cruisers Nachi (Rear-Admiral Takagi) and Haguro, the light cruisers Naka (Nishimura) and Jintsu, and 13 destroyers.

Though the Allies thus had a numerical superiority in cruisers, the range at which the action opened, more than 13 miles, meant that it was the numbers of 8-inch guns involved that was the critical factor. And here the Japanese prevailed, with 20 such weapons against the Allies' 12 (it should be remembered that Houston had been hit by bombs on February 4, and this had knocked out her after turret). The battle was to continue for almost seven hours without achieving concrete results, partly because the Japanese were more concerned with the safety of their convoy than sinking Allied vessels, and partly because the Allied warships had no reconnaissance aircraft, and were thus forced, as Morison puts it, to play a kind of blind man's bluff.

During the first engagement, Exeter was hit in her engine room at 1708 and hauled out of the line, the cruisers following her doing the same under the impression that such a manoeuvre had been ordered by Doorman in De Ruyter, leading the Allied line. While the crippled British cruiser made for Surabaja, the Japanese launched a wave of 72 torpedoes, only one of which, remarkably, hit an Allied warship, the Dutch destroyer Kortenaer, which exploded and sank. While covering the retirement of Exeter, the British destroyer Electra was stopped by gunfire and hammered into a blazing wreck. During the night, Doorman searched in vain for the Japanese convoy, which had been ordered by Nishimura to retreat to the north during the action, without finding it. He was also forced to release his American destroyers, which had expended all their torpedoes and were running drastically short of fuel.

During his fruitless search for the Japanese transports, however, Doorman once again ran into their escort, in the form of the cruiser Jintsu and her seven destroyers, at 1930. Turning away from the Japanese cruiser, Doorman inadvertently led his force over a newly-laid Dutch minefield, which cost him the British destroyer Jupiter. But time was running out for the Allied ships, for Japanese seaplanes had been keeping their cruisers informed of the Allied survivors' movements, and Nachi and Haguro were moving in for the kill. During the subsequent engagement, De Ruyter and Java were both hit and sunk by Japanese torpedoes. Doorman went down with his flagship. Immediately afterwards Perth and Houston broke off the action and returned to Batavia.

The crisis in Allied naval fortunes had yet further to run, however. After refuelling at Batavia, Perth and Houston received orders to retire southwards through the Sunda Strait. Here they ran into the second of the Japanese convoys mentioned above. This had sailed from Indo-China and was in the process of landing the first units of the Japanese 2nd Division in Banten Bay. The two Allied cruisers immediately went into the attack, and managed to sink one transport and force three others to beach themselves, as well as damaging one cruiser and three destroyers, before being sunk by the rest of the Japanese escort.

A few hours later, Exeter sailed from Surabaja with two destroyers to try to pass through the Sunda Strait. They were spotted by Japanese reconnaissance aircraft and sunk by four cruisers and three destroyers on March 1.

Defeat in Java

The naval defeat of February 27 sealed the fate of Java. The two vital centres of Batavia and Surabaja fell into Imamura's hands, and General ter Poorten asked the Japanese commander for armistice terms. As was to be expected, the victor demanded unconditional surrender, which he received at Bandung on March 10. Sherwood notes at this time:

"Churchill, who had won his greatest Parliamentary triumph a scant three weeks before, now faced the worst predicament of his career as Prime Minister. He made a broadcast speech in which he attributed the whole series of misfortunes in the Far East to the fact that America's shield of sea power had been 'dashed to the ground' at Pearl Harbor. There were numerous expressions of irritation at this statement in Washington, as though Churchill were attempting to escape censure by blaming it all on the U.S. Navy, but it did not bother Roosevelt at all. He merely remarked: 'Winston had to say something.'"

Retreat to Singapore

Under the keen and vigorous command of Lieutenant-General Tomoyuki Yamashita, the Japanese 25th Army smashed its way through the British defences in the north of Malaya. On January 1, 1942 Kuantan, on the east coast, fell to the swiftly-advancing Japanese, while on the other side of the country Kuala Lumpur, on the Slim river, succumbed on the 11th, after a period of fierce resistance. Seeing his reserves melting away, Percival ordered his forces to fall back on Singapore on January 29, after asking for and receiving Wavell's authorisation. On January 30 the causeway linking the island fortress and the mainland was blown up.

But Singapore's garrison, its back to the wall, was in no position to offer a solid resistance for the great imperial base, which was intended to close the Indian Ocean to attack from the east and to ensure the safety of Britain's sea link with Australia and New Zealand. The Committee of Imperial Defence had recognised since the mid-1930's that the survival of Singapore in the face of a land attack depended upon the successful defence of the jungles of the Malayan hinterland — and that a Japanese attack via Malaya was quite probable. But now that the British defence of Malaya had collapsed, Singapore was practically indefensible.

In his memoirs, Churchill tells us of the "feelings of painful surprise" he had when reading Wavell's message of January 16, which emphasised Singapore's weakness as a fortress. Churchill adds:

"Moreover, even more astounding, no measures worth speaking of had been taken by any of the commanders since the war began, and more especially since the Japanese had established themselves in Indo-China, to construct field defences. They had not even mentioned the fact they did not exist." He summed up as follows:

"I do not write this in any way to excuse myself. I ought to have known. My advisers ought to have known and I ought to have been told, and ought to have asked. The reason I had not asked about this matter, amid the thousands of questions I put, was that the possibility of Singapore having no landward defences no more entered into my mind than that of a battleship being launched without a bottom." It should be added, however, that Churchill had been a member of the Conservative cabinet in the 1920's when the Singapore base was planned and begun. There is, therefore, no reason why he should not have known the details

then.

The fall of Singapore

In the circumstances, it was not difficult for General Yamashita, on the night of February 8–9, to get his forces across the Strait of Johore and win a beach-head north-west of the city of Singapore. Immediately afterwards, the Japanese captured Tengah airfield and the reservoirs supplying the city's million inhabitants with water.

On February 15, the advanced guard of the Japanese 5th Division ran into the British delegation sent out to seek terms for surrender. General Yamashita refused to discuss terms, but insisted that General Percival come to see him personally. The Japanese commander told Percival that his forces "respect the valour of your army and will honour your dead", but then insisted on unconditional surrender. Percival hesitated for nearly an hour, and then signed the British surrender.

One of Yamashita's staff then asked if he was to prepare for a victory parade through the streets of Singapore, to which he received the dry reply:

"No. The war isn't finished. We have lost 3,300 men in the campaign. What have the survivors done to deserve it? We must first honour our dead. Then we'll prepare for future campaigns."

The disaster in Malaya provoked another crisis between the irritable Mr. Curtin and Churchill, following on their earlier disagreement about Tobruk.

Curtin had a majority of two in the Australian parliament and stubbornly refused to introduce the conscription necessary for the defence of Australia. This did not, however, prevent him from abusing Churchill for his lack of zeal in calling the home country to the defence of her Pacific dominions. On December 27, 1941, for example, the following virtual ultimatum appeared over Curtin's signature in the Melbourne Herald:

"Without any inhibitions of any kind, I make it quite clear that Australia looks to America, free of any pangs as to our traditional links with the United Kingdom.

"We know the problems that the United Kingdom faces. We know the constant threat of invasion. We know the dangers of dispersal of strength. But we know too that Australia can go, and Britain can still hold on.

"We are therefore determined that Australia shall not go, and we shall exert all our energies towards the shaping of a plan, with the United States as its keystone, which will give to our country some confidence of being able to hold out until the tide of battle swings against the enemy.

"Summed up, Australian external policy will be shaped towards obtaining Russian aid, and working out, with the United States, as the major factor, a plan of Pacific strategy, along with British, Chinese, and Dutch forces."

The reader will be spared the details of the somewhat acrimonious correspondence which followed. In the course of this the Australian Prime Minister went so far as to inform his British opposite number that after all the assurances that had been given to various Canberra governments for years: "the evacuation of Singapore would be regarded here and elsewhere as an inexcusable betrayal."

Japanese troops parading in Raffles square after the fall of Singapore.

But it must be emphasised that Churchill, for all his normal impetuosity, made no attempt to modify his attitude to placate the Australian Prime Minister. Faced with the daily-growing threat of the Japanese advance, it was decided to withdraw the 6th and 7th Australian Divisions from the Middle East and incorporate them into the defence of Java and what British and American strategists called the "Malay barrier", separating the Indian Ocean from the Pacific.

Japanese soldiers celebrate victory - Limay, Bataan.

Meanwhile, the defence of the Philippines had been concentrated in the Bataan Peninsula, west of Manila Bay. Here MacArthur had 15,000 Americans and 65,000 Filipinos, although only 10,000 of the latter could be considered as fully trained soldiers. MacArthur's foresight had provided the garrison with ample ammunition, but the position with food supplies was a problem right from the beginning of the siege as the provisions for the garrison itself had to be spread to feed the thousands of refugees who had fled the Japanese advance and now seriously jeopardised the defence of Bataan. Notwithstanding, the American and Filipino forces on the peninsula held out for a very creditable period, not surrendering until April 9, 1942 after a siege of 98 days.

Bataan holds out

On January 10, Lieutenant-General Homma, the commander of the Japanese 14th Army, sent the following message to MacArthur:

"Sir,

You are well aware that you are doomed. The end is near. The question is how long you will be able to resist. You have already cut rations by half. I appreciate the fighting spirit of yourself and your troops who have been fighting with courage. Your prestige and honour have been upheld.

"However, in order to avoid needless bloodshed and to save the remnants of your divisions and your auxiliary troops, you are advised to surrender."

When this summons remained unanswered, the 14th Army

attacked the American lines during the night of the 11th. After ten days of fruitless frontal attacks, the Japanese infiltrated the American lines across the slopes of Mount Natib, which the defenders had thought inaccessible, and thus forced the Americans to fall back to their second defence line across the peninsula. The retreat was conducted in an orderly fashion, however, and the American forces did not lose their cohesion. Homma, to his extreme chagrin, had to ask Tokyo for reinforcements.

On February 22, MacArthur received a message from the White House ordering him to quit Bataan, organise the defence of Mindanao to the south, and then proceed to Australia. MacArthur delayed in executing these orders, claiming that his departure would result in the immediate collapse of resistance in the Philippines. On March 10, however, Roosevelt cabled him: "Proceed immediately to Melbourne." General MacArthur could no longer ignore this direct order, and on the night of the 11th, he and his staff sailed from his command post on the island of Corregidor in four PT boats (motor torpedo boats). After an eventful three days at sea, MacArthur landed at Cagayan de Oro in Mindanao, flying from there to Australia on board a B-17 bomber. On this occasion he made his celebrated promise to the journalists waiting for him "I shall return!"

Major-General J. M. Wainwright, who succeeded MacArthur as commander in the Philippines, visited his superior just before he left. Their conversation has been preserved by John Toland:

"'Jonathan,' [MacArthur] said as they shook hands, 'I want you to understand my position very plainly.' He was leaving he said, only because of insistent, repeated orders from Roosevelt. At first he had told his staff he would refuse, but they convinced him that defying the President's direct order would bring disciplinary action. 'I want you to make it known throughout all elements of your command that I'm leaving over my repeated protests.'

"'Of course I will, Douglas,' said Wainwright.

"'If I get through to Australia, you know I'll come back as soon as I can with as much as I can.' Then he warned of the necessity of greater defense in depth. 'And be sure to give them everything you've got with your artillery. That's the best arm you have.'

"The two men were quiet for a moment. In the distance the dull rumble of battle from Bataan could be heard. Wainwright was thinking of the dwindling ammunition and food supply, his air force of two battered P-40's, of the spreading malaria and dysentery and lack of medicine. He said, 'You'll get through.'

"'And back,' MacArthur added with determination. He gave Wainwright a box of cigars and two large jars of shaving cream. 'Good-bye Jonathan.' They shook hands warmly. 'If you're still on Bataan when I get back, I'll make you a Lieutenant-General.'

"'I'll be on Bataan if I'm still alive.' Wainwright turned and slowly started back to his lunch."

Surrender on Bataan

When he arrived in Australia, General MacArthur, who had been eating at the same mess as his men, noted that he had lost nearly two stones in weight at Bataan. It is thus clear that the American garrison was severely weakened when Homma launched his final assault. Added to this physical debilitation was the loss of morale of the troops, to whom it was now abundantly clear

Surrender at Bataan - US soldiers file past Japanese troops.

sent emissaries to the Japanese to discuss terms on April 9. The surrender was signed the next day; 64,000 Filipinos and 12,000 Americans were taken prisoner.

The Bataan "Death March"

There then followed the notorious "Death March", when the prisoners taken on Bataan were marched from Mariveles 55 miles to the railhead at San Fernando, under the most inhuman conditions. During the march, 2,330 Americans and between 7–10,000 Filipinos died. As the officer responsible, General Homma was tried after the war, found guilty, and executed. General MacArthur, turning down a final appeal for Homma, said: "I am again confronted with the repugnant duty of passing final judgement on a former adversary in a major military campaign … I approve the finding of guilt and direct the Commanding General, United States Forces in the Western Pacific to execute the sentence."

But the American historian John Toland examined all the documents pertaining to the case and did not come to such definite conclusions about Homma's guilt, attaching blame more to the 14th Army's general staff for their irresponsibility than to Homma himself for criminal intent. The Japanese had expected to find 30,000 prisoners and got 76,000, all of them in poor physical condition. Twenty miles from Mariveles, transport had been provided for the rest of the journey, but only 230 trucks were available. Moreover, the behaviour of the Japanese guards towards their prisoners varied considerably: in some cases it was relatively humane, in others completely abominable. This seems to indicate

that there was no possibility of a relief force reaching them. These facts, then, make it clear why General Wainwright was unable to galvanise his men to action. Moreover, the Japanese 14th Army had been reinforced with another division and brigade, and had improved its tactics, from now on combining frontal assaults with small-scale landings in the Americans' rear.

On April 1 Wainwright ignored a fresh summons from Homma to surrender and accept an "honourable defeat". The final Japanese attack started two days later, and three days after that the American defences were finally breached. After the failure of one counter-attack, General King, commanding on Bataan, considered that his men were at the end of their tether and

March of death from Bataan to Cabana Philippines.

that these guards were not obeying a general directive from their superiors.

The end in the Philippines

The Japanese now controlled all of Luzon except the island fortress of Corregidor and the islets surrounding it. While the Americans held these, the Japanese were denied the use of Manila harbour. On May 4, the Japanese poured a barrage of 16,000 shells on to the island, and under the cover so provided landed a powerful assault force, which managed to secure a small beach-head. The American garrison numbered 15,000, but of these only 1,300 could be considered battleworthy. Homma urged Wainwright to surrender, but insisted that if he did so, the

capitulation must also apply to all other American forces in the Philippines archipelago. The Japanese would thus be able to secure Mindanao and the islands around the Visayan Sea without firing a shot.

After a painful mental struggle, and despite MacArthur's intervention, Wainwright finally ordered his subordinates to terminate their resistance. The latter at first protested, but all American resistance finally ended on May 6, 1942. Wainwright was not condemned for ordering the capitulation by the American Government, General Marshall, and MacArthur. Indeed, with General Percival, who had surrendered Singapore, he was one of those invited to the Japanese surrender ceremony on September 2, 1945.

The turn of Burma

According to Churchill, it was not expected in London that the Japanese would invade Burma until they had finished with Malaya and conquered Singapore. As a result of this lack of foresight, the defences of this wealthy colony were extremely sparse. On December 8, 1941 they comprised troops totalling about a division — the 1st Burma Division, Burmese battalions stiffened by two British battalions and an Indian brigade. Towards the end of January 1942, the incomplete 17th Indian Division was shipped in. The whole was under Major-General T. J. Hutton. The R.A.F. was in an even worse position, with only four Bristol Blenheim light bombers and 32 superannuated Brewster Buffalo fighters, of which only 24 were airworthy.

Burma was as important to the Japanese as Malaya or India,

not only for its oil and other natural resources, but because it contained the "Burma Road", which had only recently been completed and linked Lashio in Burma with Chungking in China. As President Roosevelt had just extended Lend-Lease to Nationalist China, the Japanese High Command considered it vital to sever this only artery supplying Generalissimo Chiang Kaishek's forces with war supplies from the "arsenal of democracy". The task of destroying this link was entrusted to the 15th Army, under Lieutenant-General S. Iida.

The invaders also had aid in Burma in the form of a large number of agents, whom the Japanese had been enlisting for years. The British knew of this, and on January 18, 1942 arrested the Prime Minister, U Saw. On the same day the Japanese 15th Army took the port and airfield of Tavoy in the south and moved on Moulmein, at the mouth of the Salween. This river, which formed a considerable natural barrier, did not slow the Japanese for long. Moulmein fell on the 31st, and the Japanese pushed on towards the Sittang. The critical phase of the campaign was reached when the Japanese arrived at this river before the retreating 17th Indian Division, under the command of Major-General J. Smyth, V.C. The bridge the division was to have used was blown prematurely, resulting in the loss of two-thirds of the division's men, most of its transport, and all its artillery to the Japanese. This defeat, on February 22, decided the campaign.

Trouble with Australia again

After the fall of Singapore, it had been decided, with the agreement of the Dutch Government, that the 6th and 7th Australian Divisions, which had previously been allocated to the defence of Java and Sumatra, should return to their own country. As the convoy in which the two divisions was sailing was off Ceylon at the time of the attack on Burma, Churchill wished to divert one, if not both, of them to Rangoon. The only result was another rebuff from Mr. Curtin on February 23:

"4. With A.I.F. troops we sought to save Malaya and Singapore, falling back on Netherlands East Indies. All these northern defences are gone or going. Now you contemplate using the A.I.F. to save Burma. All this has been done, as in Greece, without adequate air support.

"5. We feel a primary obligation to save Australia not only for itself, but to preserve it as a base for the development of the war against Japan. In the circumstances it is quite impossible to reverse a decision which we made with the utmost care, and which we have affirmed and reaffirmed."

In this situation there can be no question but that the Australian Prime Minister was right. In so critical a situation, Churchill and the Combined Chiefs-of-Staff Committee would only have been writing off the division or divisions that ventured into this hopeless theatre of operations.

On March 5, 1942, General Sir Harold Alexander arrived from England to take over command in Burma from Hutton. The decision to send out a new commander was, to some extent, quite understandable. Alexander was an optimistic and determined officer, but within a short time of his arrival realised that he was faced by problems very similar to those which he had met at Dunkirk.

US surrender, Philippine islands, generals Wainwright and Horuna.

Rangoon abandoned

The capital of Burma was defended by the remnants of the 17th Indian Division, while the 1st Burma Division, made up of native battalions with British and Indian strengthening, was operating against the invaders to the north. But the defenders were so short of men that a 125-mile gap had opened up between the two divisions, and through this the Japanese were infiltrating in considerable numbers. At first Alexander ordered that Rangoon must be held, but then came to Hutton's view that British forces were too weak for this task. He therefore decided to concentrate his troops for the defence of Upper Burma, and the retreat began. Rangoon was abandoned on March 7, the British retreating up the Irrawaddy valley to regroup their forces, now reinforced by the arrival of the British 7th Armoured Brigade, more infantry, and aerial reinforcements from Britain and China. Lieutenant-General William Slim was appointed to command these reorganised forces.

Alexander now decided that his primary strategic objective was the protection of the Yenangyaung oilfields, in which he was to be aided by the Chinese 5th and 6th Armies, under the command of Lieutenant-General "Vinegar Joe" Joseph Stilwell, the American officer who had been considered originally for the command of Operation "Super-Gymnast" but was now Chiang Kai-shek's military right hand. But co-operation with the Chinese proved difficult. A force equivalent in size to a British division was considered an army, and Chinese tactics bore very little resemblance either to Allied or Japanese ones. The following anecdote from Field-Marshal Lord Alexander's memoirs will serve to illustrate this:

"Before the battle of Mandalay I went round the front to inspect our defences and was much impressed to see how cleverly this Chinese Fifth Army had dug in its field guns, which were well sited and cleverly camouflaged. When contact had been gained with the advancing Japanese I again visited the front, and to my astonishment I found that the artillery had disappeared.

"When I asked the army commander what had happened to his guns he said that he had withdrawn them to safety.

"'Then you mean,' I said, 'that they will take no part in the battle?'

"'Exactly,' he replied.

"'But then what use are they?'

"He said: 'General, the Fifth Chinese Army is our best army, because it is the only one which has any field guns, and I cannot afford to risk those guns. If I lose them the Fifth Army will no longer be our best.'"

Retreat to India

In the circumstances, upper Burma was no more defensible than lower Burma. The Japanese 15th Army had been reinforced by two more divisions and more aircraft just before the capture of Rangoon, and the British-Chinese line south of Mandalay had not the resources to hold the Japanese advance. In the middle of April the Japanese took Yenangyaung, though the Allies managed

-to sabotage the oil wells before they arrived. At the end of the month, on the 29th, the Japanese drove the Chinese 5th Army back over the border into China and occupied Lashio. Alexander, with his left flank exposed by the defeat of the Chinese, was forced to evacuate Mandalay, and retreat towards India across the Irrawaddy and Chindwin rivers. When the monsoon began, his little army was safe in the Indian state of Manipur after the longest, and one of the most gruelling, retreats ever carried out by the British Army.

The Japanese capped their victory in Burma by occupying the Andaman Islands, in which Port Blair offered them an excellent anchorage.

Lieutenant-General Joseph W. Stilwell was nominated by Roosevelt as chief-of-staff and general military adviser to Chiang Kai-shek, and arrived in Burma in February 1942. Thus his first experience of fighting the Japanese was the ultimate test of any general: fighting a retreat. He threw himself into the task of training the Chinese forces, and of instilling fighting spirit into Chiang and his generals. He had a thankless and frustrating job, way down on the list of Allied priorities.

Nagumo's successes

The above advances by the Japanese land forces were matched by the successes of Vice-Admiral Chuichi Nagumo's Carrier Fleet. On January 20, planes from Nagumo's carriers bombed Rabaul on New Britain, and then this extremely important strategic point in the South-West Pacific was captured on the 23rd. Possession of this base gave the Japanese the choice of advancing either on

New Guinea or the Solomons. On February 29, Japanese carrier-borne aircraft raided Port Darwin, on the north coast of Australia, sinking a dozen merchantmen in the harbour. A few days later, the Carrier Fleet was ordered to move south of Java, with the aim of preventing the evacuation of the island when the Japanese invaded from the north. Between March 3 and 5, repeated attacks were made on the port of Tjilatjap, causing the loss of three destroyers and 17 transports. On March 26, the Carrier Fleet sailed from Kendari, under the command of Vice-Admiral Kondo, to launch a surprise attack against targets on the island of Ceylon.

The Japanese fleet sent on this mission was a powerful one: five aircraft-carriers (with some 300 aircraft), four Kongo-class battleships (14-inch guns), two heavy cruisers, one light cruiser, and eight destroyers. As this force attacked Ceylon, another squadron, comprising the light aircraft-carrier Ryujo, six cruisers, and eight destroyers, was to carry out a raid in the Bay of Bengal, under the command of Vice-Admiral Ozawa. British reconnaissance aircraft had seen the beginning of this two-pronged attack, and the British War Cabinet became intensely worried lest the Japanese should try to obtain naval and air superiority in the Indian Ocean.

Britain's Eastern Fleet

The question had, in fact, been discussed by the Japanese. In order to take maximum advantage of their recent run of brilliant successes, this strategic aim appeared to be both possible and appropriate. Captain Kuroshima, head of the operations section of the Combined Fleet headquarters, supported the idea. In his

US surrender at Corrgidor.

opinion, it was advisable to make use of the respite gained by the neutralisation of the American forces in the Pacific to crush the British squadron in the Indian Ocean, conquer Ceylon, and advance on the Red Sea and Persian Gulf. The Japanese forces would then advance to meet their Axis partners sweeping down from the Caucasus and east from Suez.

Realising that this possibility was on the way to becoming a probability after the fall of Malaya, Admiral of the Fleet Sir Dudley Pound made every effort to frustrate this dangerous scheme. To this end he assembled in the area of Ceylon the elements of a new fleet, under Admiral Sir James Somerville, the former commander of Force H at Gibraltar. On the day that

Corregidor - post war remains - 12in mortar battery.

Kondo and Ozawa sailed from Kendari, the Eastern Fleet, as the new British fleet was called, consisted of three aircraft-carriers (Indomitable, Formidable, and the aged Hermes), five battleships (Warspite, which had just returned from repairs in the U.S.A., and the four Royal Sovereign-class vessels, with a total of 40 15-inch guns), two heavy cruisers, five light cruisers (one of them Dutch), 16 destroyers, and seven submarines (two of them Dutch).

On his way out to take up his new command, Somerville wrote to Pound a masterly appreciation of the situation in the Indian Ocean: if the Japanese captured Ceylon "it will be extremely difficult, but not necessarily impossible, to maintain our communications to the Middle East. But if the Japanese capture Ceylon and destroy the greater part of the Eastern Fleet, then … the situation becomes really desperate."

The British had learnt the lessons of the loss of Prince of Wales and Repulse, and now had a better appreciation than before of the relative strengths of the forces which might come into contact. Somerville realistically decided that it could not be in the Royal Navy's favour. Admittedly, the British fleet's 40 15-inch guns were superior to Kondo's 32 14-inch weapons, but to use this advantage, the four Royal Sovereigns would have to maintain contact with the Kongos, which were five knots faster. Yet more important was the question of defence. The British ships had been built in World War I and had been little modified, resulting in inadequate deck armour and A.A. armament. The Japanese naval aircraft, which were in every respect superior to their British counterparts, would have made short work of them.

Somerville had only about 100 out-of-date bombers and fighters to put up against more than 300 superior Japanese machines, which also had excellent crews. This disparity was clearly shown in an engagement off Colombo on April 5, when a formation of 12 Fairey Swordfish torpedo-bombers was surprised by Japanese Zeros and completely destroyed. On April 1, Somerville divided his fleet into two parts. The faster and more effective part, Force A, was to go on patrol, using Addu Attol, a new secret base in the Maldive Islands about 600 miles south-west of Ceylon, to refuel. The British fleet avoided exposure either to a fleet action or to air attacks, unable to match the superior striking power of the Japanese carrier force. The British position in the Indian Ocean was now seriously threatened.

Hermes sunk

Colombo was bombed on April 5, though the raid missed the cruisers Cornwall and Dorsetshire, which had sailed late on the

4th. On the morning of the 5th, however, they were spotted by Japanese aircraft. An attack by 80 planes was swiftly mounted, and under a rain of bombs (about 90 per cent hit their targets) the two heavy cruisers sank. On April 9 Hermes, which had been launched in 1919 and was one of the world's oldest aircraft-carriers, was caught by a raid as she was leaving Trincomalee harbour with the Australian destroyer Vampire. Both vessels were sunk. At the same time, Ozawa was attacking merchant shipping further to the north, where he sank 23 vessels, displacing a total of 112,312 tons. In the first ten days of the month, Japanese submarines operating in the area sank a further 32,404 tons. To the south again, the British were fortunate in evading Nagumo's aircraft, which were searching south-east of Ceylon, whereas the British fleet was in fact to the west of the island.

On April 7, however, the British Admiralty realised that the Japanese had not been deterred from advancing into the Indian Ocean by the Allied forces there, and authorised Somerville to withdraw to East Africa. Somerville decided to send his slower ships there while he himself, with the faster units, continued in the area. The withdrawal of the British fleet was a further humiliation for British seapower. Fortunately for the Allies, however, the Japanese forces did not exploit their opportunity, having already strayed beyond the limits they had set themselves beforehand.

So the crisis soon passed. On April 12 the Japanese Combined Fleet had returned to Kure to prepare for its next offensive operations. Kondo and Ozawa returned to the Pacific, and major Japanese units never again entered the Indian Ocean.

Japan at high tide

This marked the end of the first phase of Japan's military expansion in World War II. General Tojo had occupied the "South-East Asia Co-Prosperity Sphere" which had been his major objective since coming to power. And he had obtained it at little cost: five destroyers, eight submarines, and 50,000 tons of merchant shipping at sea; and 10,000 dead and 4,000 wounded on land.

The Japanese advance into the Indian Ocean had presented the Allied command with the question of how to deal with the Vichy French colony of Madagascar, in particular the naval base at Diego-Suarez in the far north of the island. As long as Churchill hoped to persuade Marshal Pétain and Admiral Darlan to support Operation "Gymnast", 'he turned a deaf ear to General de Gaulle's exhortations to him to occupy Madagascar. But Rommel's success in Cyrenaica postponed any landing in North Africa indefinitely.

Laval's return to power, on the other hand, raised Allied fears that Vichy might agree to hand over Madagascar, which controls the Moçambique Channel, to the Japanese. Churchill decided to wait no longer, and Operation "Ironclad" was launched on May 5, when naval and land forces under Rear-Admiral E. N. Syfret and Major-General R. C. Sturges captured Diego-Suarez. Further landings were made between September 10 and 29, resulting in the surrender of the final Vichy forces on November 6.

In fact the Japanese had no real interest in the Indian Ocean, and the invasion of Madagascar did nothing but remove a threat that never existed and further exacerbate relations between Vichy and Great Britain.

Douglas Dauntless planes onboard USS Yorktown during the Battle of Coral Sea.

Admiral Chester Nimitz was born in Texas in 1885. He served in World War I as Chief-of-Staff to the Commander of the U.S. Atlantic Submarine Force, and after Pearl Harbor he was made Commander-in-Chief of the Pacific Fleet. His victories at the battles of Coral Sea and Midway crippled the Japanese fleet and assured the safety of the United States from direct naval attack.

The question of whether the neutralisation of the American aero-naval forces based on Pearl Harbor should be exploited by a landing on the island of Oahu was discussed in Tokyo during the detailed planning for the December 7 attack. The answer had been "no". Those responsible for Japanese strategy were content

with knocking out the main U.S. fleet, thus gaining the time necessary for their forces to overrun South-East Asia. After that they would consider the matter again.

And so, after the capture of Guam and Wake, in the south-eastern Pacific theatre, the Japanese contented themselves with the occupation of the Gilbert Islands, on which they based their major defensive hopes.

Pearl Harbor was a fatal blow to Operation "Rainbow", the American conquest of the Marshall and the Caroline Islands and the organisation of an American base at Truk. The Pacific Fleet had had an offensive mission; now it was on the defensive, but this was only for the time being and there was no danger that it would become a passive force. This was the idea which

Rear-Admiral Husband E. Kimmel expressed in a note to Navy Secretary Knox on December 11, 1941 when the latter arrived in Pearl Harbor:

"With the losses we have sustained, it is necessary to revise completely our strategy of a Pacific war. The loss of battleships commits us to the strategic defensive until our forces can again be built up. However, a very powerful striking force of carriers, cruisers and destroyers survives. These forces must be operated boldly and vigorously on the tactical offensive in order to retrieve our initial disaster."

In support of this opinion it should be said that on that same day the Pacific Fleet still had in fighting trim the aircraft-carriers Lexington, Saratoga, and Enterprise, 16 cruisers, 44 destroyers, and 16 submarines, some at sea, others in bases at Pearl Harbor and Bremerton (Washington State). Also, when he heard of the Japanese attack, Vice-Admiral Stark, Chief of Naval Operations, ordered the Atlantic Fleet to send Yorktown, a carrier of the same class as Enterprise, through the Panama Canal to the Pacific — a vital reinforcement.

Nimitz takes over the Pacific Fleet

Scarcely had Kimmel formulated his rather optimistic plan than he was relieved of his command and replaced, on Roosevelt's personal choice, by Rear-Admiral Chester W. Nimitz: "a towhaired, blue-eyed Texan, of the Naval Academy class of 1905. Tactful and modest, sound in his judgement of men and events, he was to prove a thoroughly fortunate choice." Such is the opinion of E. B. Potter, a professor at the Annapolis Naval Academy, with whom Nimitz later wrote books on naval warfare in World War II.

On December 27 Nimitz took over as Commander-in-Chief Pacific Fleet, or Cincpac, with promotion to Admiral, whilst in Washington Admiral Ernest J. King was appointed head of the U.S. Navy, replacing Vice-Admiral Stark. King thus became Cincus, Commander-in-Chief United States Fleet, and addressed his first order to Cincpac, defining his mission in these terms:

"1) Covering and holding the Hawaii–Midway line and maintaining communications with the west coast.

2) Maintaining communications between the west coast and Australia, chiefly by covering, securing, and holding the Hawaii–Samoa line which should be extended to include Fiji at the earliest practical date."

The execution of this order postulated the setting up of an air-sea front running from Dutch Harbor (Alaska) to Midway, including New Caledonia and hinging on Port Moresby in New Guinea. Nimitz could, of course, call upon all possible facilities in the British and Australian possessions in the Pacific. The French territories had gone over to de Gaulle in the summer of 1940 and in the following year an agreement reached between the Free French leader and the American Government gave the same facilities to the Americans in the case of aggression by the Japanese. The Pacific Fleet's task, therefore, was to engage and repel all enemy forces which attempted to force the front described above. But it was not to be restricted within this perimeter. On the contrary it was, as Admiral King is said to have put it, "to hold what you've got and hit them when you can".

General Douglas MacArthur, President Franklin D Roosevelt, Admiral Chester W Nimitz aboard USS Baltimore.

American skirmishes

Admiral Nimitz set about his task as best he could, in spite of the temporary loss of Saratoga, damaged by a torpedo on January 11, 1942 and out of service for five months thereafter. On February 1, groups commanded by Rear-Admiral F. J. Fletcher and Vice-Admiral W. F. Halsey, each built round one carrier, "struck", the one in the Gilbert archipelago and the other in the Marshall Islands, to such effect that the Japanese High Command thought it necessary to withdraw the aircraft-carriers Zuikaku and Shokaku from the fleet then preparing to operate in the Indian Ocean. During another undertaking by Halsey, planes from Enterprise bombed Wake Island on February 24, then Marcus Island. The latter was only about 1,100 miles from the Japanese capital.

Japanese plans

Aboard the battleship Nagato, flying the flag of Admiral Yamamoto in Hiroshima Bay, the Combined Fleet's Chief-of-Staff, Rear-Admiral Ugaki, had been concerned since late January about what the next Japanese naval operations should be. In his opinion, it was important to take advantage immediately of the superiority of the naval and naval air forces enjoyed by Japan to crush the American fleet and seize Hawaii. Among the arguments which seemed to him to point to this conclusion we mention one:

"Time would work against Japan because of the vastly superior natural resources of the United States. Conse quently, unless Japan quickly resumed the offensive — the sooner the better — she eventually would become incapable of doing anything more than sitting down and waiting for the American forces to counter-attack. Furthermore, although Japan had steeled herself to endure a prolonged struggle, it would be obviously to her advantage to shorten it if at all possible, and the only hope of so doing lay in offensive action."

But Rear-Admiral Ugaki was unable to convince his Chief of Operations, Captain Kuroshima, who considered that a new attack on Hawaii would no longer have the benefit of surprise. Quite to the contrary, and a Japanese fleet operating in these waters would now have to deal not only with the enemy's naval forces but also with his air force and coastal batteries. In the face of these difficulties Kuroshima opted for an offensive westwards: the destruction of the British fleet in the Indian Ocean, the conquest of Ceylon, and the establishment of contact with the Axis powers. These were the objectives he recommended to the Japanese High Command.

Ceylon is reprieved

Direct co-operation between Japan, Germany, and Italy soon had to be abandoned as the links between the three totalitarian allies were very tenuous. Kuroshima's proposal was nevertheless examined very carefully both by Admiral Yamamoto and at the highest level of the Naval General Staff by Admiral Nagano. This was the state of things in late February when the Army, under the pretext of the Soviet pressure on Manchukuo, refused their co-operation in any attack on Ceylon.

Meanwhile the headquarters of the Combined Fleet had been set up on board the giant battleship Yamato. Here Ugaki's arguments against any expectations of assistance seemed still to prevail. So, turned away from Ceylon by the Army's unwillingness, no time was lost in turning the offensive eastwards. Account was taken of the objections against a direct attack on Hawaii and it was therefore decided to mount an operation for the capture of Midway. This objective was far enough away from Oahu to prevent interference by land-based American aircraft; it was also important enough to compel the enemy fleet to fight, and without land-based support this would allow the Japanese battleships and aircraft-carriers to use their as yet undoubted superiority.

Admiral Yamamoto approved the plan submitted to him for the attack on Midway and sent it forward on April 2 for approval by the Naval High Command. But in Tokyo, among Nagano's colleagues, it ran into opposition from the Operations Section, where Admiral Fukudome was insisting on an attack against Australia. According to Commander Fuchida, whose account of the matter we have drawn on, the "Australian School", as the supporters of an offensive in this area were called, put forward the following arguments:

"Australia, because of its size and strategic location on the Japanese defensive perimeter, would almost certainly become the springboard for an eventual Allied counter-offensive. This counteroffensive, they reasoned, would be spearheaded by air power in order to take full advantage of American industrial capacity to produce planes by mass-production methods, and the effective utilisation of this massive air strength would require the use of land bases in Australia. Consequently, there would be a weak spot in Japan's defensive armour unless Australia were either placed under Japanese control or effectively cut off from the United States."

It is true that the Army had refused the Navy the one division thought necessary to overrun Ceylon, and it had all the more reason to refuse to put ten into an operation such as this. They would content themselves, therefore, with isolating Australia and this would be done by the progressive occupation of New Guinea, the Solomon Islands, New Caledonia, New Hebrides, Fiji, and Samoa.

The "Doolittle Raid"

Admiral Yamamoto did not agree with this line of reasoning. In his opinion the G.H.Q. plan would not give him the great naval battle which he thought so necessary for swift victory. Admiral Nagano supported him, though very much against his better judgement. These differences of opinion continued up to the day of the operation, but on April 18 an event occurred which cut short all discussion: the bombing of Tokyo by a handful of North American B-25 Mitchell twin-engined bombers under the command of Lieutenant-Colonel James H. Doolittle.

These planes weighed 13 tons fully loaded and nothing so heavy had ever taken off from an aircraft-carrier before. Lengthy preparations were therefore necessary. On April 13 the aircraft-carrier Hornet, with 16 of these B-25's on board, rendezvoused with Task Force 16, under Halsey, which was to escort her. The plan was that Doolittle and his companions were to take off some 500 miles from Japan, carry out their mission, and land in Nationalist China, deck landings by B-25's being impossible. Some 200 miles east of the area from which the planes were to take off, Halsey's force fell in with an enemy patrol and the American admiral had to order Doolittle to take off at once as the necessary secrecy could no longer be guaranteed.

A few tons of bombs were shared out between the Japanese capital and the large cities of Nagoya and Kobe from 1300 hours on April 13, and no appreciable damage was done. But nonetheless the psychological impact of Doolittle's raiders on the Japanese people and on the Japanese armed forces was immense. The Emperor's own palace had been exposed to the danger of a direct attack. The Imperial Armed Forces' loss of face had to be made good.

Of the 16 twin-engined B-25s which took part in the raid, one landed on the aerodrome at Vladivostok and was seized by the Soviet authorities. The pilots of the remaining 15, running out of fuel, either crash landed or ordered their crews to bale out. Of the 80 crew, five were interned by the Russians, 62 were picked up by the Chinese, one was killed while descending by parachute, four drowned, and eight were taken prisoner by the Japanese. Three of these last were executed as "war criminals".

In the face of this air-raid, which was the bitterest humiliation for the whole Navy, there was no further disagreement over Yamamoto's plan. He offered his personal excuses to the Emperor. The Admiral was incensed by the American raid and he was bent

Gen. Doolittle poses with crew & Chinese guides.

on destroying the U.S. Pacific fleet by advancing to Hawaii. So on May 5 the Chief of Naval Operations issued "Naval Order No. 18 of the Grand Imperial Headquarters" requiring that before June 20 the Commander of the Combined Fleet should "proceed to the occupation of Midway Island and key positions in the Western Aleutians in collaboration with the army".

Meanwhile the 4th Fleet (Vice-Admiral Inouye), suitably reinforced, was to occupy Port Moresby on the south coast of eastern New Guinea and the little island of Tulagi in the Solomon archipelago opposite Guadalcanal. At the beginning of July they were expected to seize strategic points in New Caledonia and Fiji. As we shall see, the "Australian School" had not given up its preferences, but Yamamoto took no notice, as meanwhile the conquest of Midway would give him the chance to wipe out the American fleet.

In April, at its base in Truk in the Caroline Islands, the Japanese 4th Fleet had been reinforced by two heavy cruisers and three aircraft-carriers, two fleet ones (Zuikaku and Shokaku, 25,700 tons each) and one small (Shoho, 11,300 tons). Acting on orders received, Vice-Admiral Shigeyoshi Inouye divided his Task Force "MO", based on the 4th Fleet, into a Carrier Striking Force, two Invasion Groups, a Support Group, and a Covering Group. The Tulagi Invasion Group occupied its objective without opposition on May 3. On the following day 14 transports of the Port Moresby Invasion Group set sail.

Moresby reinforced

Under an agreement of March 17 between London and Washington, the United States had agreed to take charge of the defence of the whole of the Pacific, including Australia and New Zealand. Alerted in time by his code-breakers, Admiral Nimitz sent Task Force 17 (Rear-Admiral Fletcher) towards Port Moresby. The force was centred on two aircraft-carriers, Yorktown (Rear-Admiral Fletcher) and Lexington (Rear-Admiral A. W. Fitch) and was joined south of the Solomon Islands by an Australian task force of cruisers under Rear-Admiral J. C. Crace. The fact remains, however, that for the accomplishment of his mission Cincpac had no authority over the 300 American planes based in northern Australia and Port Moresby. These were under the Supreme Commander South-West Asia, General MacArthur, and hence there was a certain lack of coordination.

The ensuing actions between the opposing forces on May 6–8 came to be called the Battle of the Coral Sea. We have already remarked that the engagement marks a date in naval warfare as it was the first time that two fleets fought from over the horizon without ever being in sight of each other, and attempted to destroy each other by bombs and aerial torpedoes.

The eminent naval historian Professor Morison has called this action the "Battle of Naval Errors". He cannot be gainsaid, in view of the many mistakes committed by the airmen on both sides, errors both in navigation and in the identification of the enemy's ships, as well as in the assessment of aerial bombing and torpedoing. In their defence, however, it must be pointed out that rapidly alternating sunshine and heavy squalls over the Coral Sea could not have made their task easy. Tactically, success went to the Japanese, since against the loss of the light carrier Shoho, one destroyer, one minelayer, and three minesweepers, they sank the American Lexington (36,000 tons), the oiler Neosho, which they took for another aircraft-carrier, and the destroyer Sims.

"The Yorktown, which came first under attack, successfully evaded the torpedoes launched at her and took only a single bomb hit, which did not significantly impair her fighting effectiveness. But the Lexington, larger and less manoeuvrable, fell victim to an 'anvil' attack on both bows simultaneously and took two torpedoes on the port side, which flooded three boiler rooms. Two bomb hits, received at almost the same time, inflicted only minor damage. The list caused by the torpedo hits was quickly corrected by shifting oil. Her engines were unharmed, and her speed did not fall below 24 knots.

"But at 1445 there was a severe explosion. Fires passed rapidly out of control and the carrier was forced to call for assistance. The Yorktown took aboard the Lexington's planes that were airborne, but there was no opportunity to transfer those already on the Lexington. With the ship burning furiously and shaken by frequent explosions there was no choice but to 'get the men off'."

Strategically, however, the advantage was on the Allies' side, as the serious damage done to Shokaku and the losses of the aircraft from Zuikaku forced Inouye to give up the idea of landing at Port Moresby.

Worse still, the several Task Forces of the Combined Fleet had to set off for Midway and the Aleutians by May 26 and it was not possible, in the short time available, either to repair Shokaku or to replace the aircraft lost by Zuikaku. On the other hand, the Japanese grossly exaggerated their successes. They claimed that Yorktown had met the same fate as Lexington, whereas she had been hit by only one 800-lb bomb. Hence the "spirit of imprudence and error" which seized Yamamoto. This is shown by the war game, or map exercise, carried out to check on Operation "Midway". The director of the exercise,

Rear-Admiral Ugaki, did not hesitate to cancel such decisions by the referee as seemed to him unfavourable to the Japanese side.

However, until the ships yet to be built under the American budgets of 1939 to 1941 came into service, the Japanese fleet enjoyed considerable superiority over its enemy. This is shown in the table at right, in which we give only the ships which took part in the actions of June 3–6 between Midway Atoll and Dutch Harbor in the Aleutians.

The Japanese aircraft-carriers had between them 410 planes, those of Admiral Nimitz 233. But Nimitz could also call upon the 115 concentrated on the airstrips at Midway in case of enemy attack. Yet these figures must not make us lose sight of the fact that the American inferiority in ships and planes was not only quantitative but qualitative as well. The Grumann F4F Wildcat fighters were less manoeuvrable and had a slower rate of climb than the Japanese Mitsubishi A6M Zeros. The torpedo bomber then in service with the U.S. Navy, the Douglas TBD-1 Devastator, with a top speed of only 206 mph, was entirely at the mercy of the Zero, Japan's standard carrier-borne fighter, which could reach some 340 mph. Also, the American air-dropped 21-inch torpedo was so slow to reach its target that the victim had

Rescued crew of the US Carrier Lexington.

a good chance of taking avoiding action. It is nevertheless true that the Japanese Commander-in-Chief threw away recklessly the enormous chances which, for the last time, his numerical and matériel superiority gave him.

A Japanese Nakajima B59 after being shot by anti-aircraft fire from a US Battleshiup.

For the operation designed to seize the islands of Attu and Kiska in the Aleutians, Yamamoto assembled a task force whose lavish size was out of all proportion to the strategic value of the objective: three heavy cruisers, three light cruisers, 13 destroyers, and the aircraft-carriers Ryujo and Junyo with between them 82 planes on board. In view of the impending threat to this theatre, however, the Americans sent out five cruisers and 13 destroyers (Task Force 8) under Rear-Admiral R. A. Theobald.

But there was a very serious and fundamental defect in the Japanese plan for the Midway operation. The Combined Fleet was split up into a number of separate task forces. They were deployed at considerable distances from each other, but the plan called on them to operate according to a rigid and complex timetable and yet to co-operate with each other in overcoming the Americans. The Japanese failed to concentrate their forces.

Admiral Yamamoto was convinced that his planned bombardment of Midway Island on June 4 and the assault on the atoll next day would provoke Nimitz into bringing out his fleet so that the engagement at sea, all being well, would take place on June 7 or 8. This would give Nagumo time to recover his liberty of action and the Japanese Commander-in-Chief to draw in his scattered forces. To leave nothing to chance, on June 2 two squadrons of submarines were to station themselves along all the routes the Americans might take on their way to assist Midway.

Logical this might have been, but there was a basic error in its reasoning, as Professor Morison has pointed out:

"The vital defect in this sort of plan is that it depends on the enemy's doing exactly what is expected. If he is smart enough to do something different — in this case to have fast carriers on the spot — the operation is thrown into confusion."

But Yamamoto, of course, had no idea that the Americans knew his movements, and could act accordingly.

Nimitz's ambush

Not counting Rear-Admiral Theobald's squadron, Admiral Nimitz's forces were divided into two groups:

1. Task Force 16, based on the aircraft-carriers Enterprise and Hornet, together with six cruisers and nine destroyers. Vice-Admiral Halsey was now in hospital and so command of this force was given to Rear-Admiral Raymond A. Spruance, whose intellectual powers were so formidable as to earn him the nickname of "electric brain".

2. Task Force 17, still under the command of Rear-Admiral F. J. Fletcher, based on the aircraft-carrier Yorktown, together with two cruisers and five destroyers. The damage sustained by Yorktown on the previous May 8 would have taken two months to repair in peacetime. The 1,400 men of the Pearl Harbor dockyard did it in less than 48 hours. This allowed Fletcher to set sail on the morning of May 30, behind Task Force 16 which had left on May 28.

And so when the Japanese submarines, which were behind schedule anyway, reached the watching stations assigned to them, Admiral Nimitz's ships had already gone, and they were thus unable to report the enemy's dispositions or strength. On June 3 at 0900 hours, when the first enemy sighting reports reached them, Fletcher and Spruance were north-east of Midway and they were in a good position to attack from the flank of the Japanese force. Leaving Pearl Harbor they had received the following warning from Cincpac in anticipation of the enemy's superior strength:

"You will be governed by the principle of calculated risk, which you shall interpret to mean the avoidance of exposure of your force to attack by superior enemy forces without good prospect of inflicting, as a result of such exposure, greater damage on the enemy."

But as Professor Potter and Admiral Nimitz point out, "to fight cautiously, to meet a superior enemy force without unduly exposing one's own is difficult in the highest degree. That Fletcher and Spruance were able to carry out these orders successfully was due primarily to their skilful exploitation of intelligence, which enabled them to turn the element of surprise against the Japanese."

Even before the Japanese fleet left its bases, Rear-Admiral Ryunosuke Kusaka, Nagumo's chief-of-staff, made the following observation to Yamamoto: so as not to hinder take-off and landing on the flight decks, the aircraft-carriers had had their masts shortened to such an extent that their radio aerials were incapable of intercepting any enemy wireless traffic. Thus the carrier forces which would be the first to make contact would be deprived of an essential source of information. It was therefore suggested that the battleship Yamato should accompany the aircraft-carriers, but this was rejected by the Commander-in-Chief.

Even so, the Japanese admiral's flagship intercepted in the single day of June 1 180 messages from Hawaii, 72 of which were classified "urgent". This sudden intensification of radio traffic, as well as the great increase in aerial reconnaissance, could mean that the enemy forces were now at sea or about to set sail. Should Nagumo, sailing on more than 600 miles ahead of Yamato, be alerted? This would mean breaking the sacrosanct radio silence and Yamamoto could not bring himself to do it, although the Americans already seemed to have penetrated the secret of Operation Midway. In such a situation the Germans would have said "Wirkung geht vor Tarnung", or "effectiveness comes before camouflage".

Battle in the sky

It was shortly after 0900 on June 3 when the first contact with the enemy was reported. A Catalina searching 470 miles to the south-west of Midway had been fired on by two Japanese patrol craft. Further confirmation that the Japanese were moving on Midway came when another Catalina spotted the convoy and escorts of the Midway Occupation Force. In Walter Lord's words:

"Farther to the west, Ensign Jack Reid piloted another PBY across an empty ocean. He had started earlier than the rest, was now 700 miles from Midway, nearing the end of his outward leg. So far, nothing worth reporting. With the PBY on automatic pilot, Reid again studied the sea with his binoculars. Still nothing — occasional cloud puffs and a light haze hung over the Pacific,

but not enough to bother him. It was shortly before 9:25 A. M., and Ensign Reid was a man with no problems at all.

"Suddenly he looked, then looked again. Thirty miles dead ahead he could make out dark objects along the horizon. Ships, lots of them, all heading toward him. Handing the glasses to his co-pilot Ensign Hardeman, he calmly asked, 'Do you see what I see?'

"Hardeman took one look: 'You are damned right I do.'

"Commander Yasumi Toyama looked up from his charts on the bridge of the light cruiser Jintsu. For once all the transports were keeping in column, but the destroyer on the port side forward was raising a fuss. She hoisted a signal, then fired a smoke shell. Toyama rushed out on the bridge wing, and there was no need to ask what had happened. Everyone was looking and pointing. There, low and well out of range on the horizon, hovered a PBY."

That afternoon the convoy was attacked from high altitude by a formation of Flying Fortresses.

At dawn Nagumo had reached a position 280 miles north-west of Midway Island. He turned his force into the wind. Then the carriers Akagi, Kaga, Hiryu, and Soryu unleashed 36 level bombers, 36 dive-bombers, and 36 fighters. At the same time six seaplanes took off to reconnoitre for American warships, followed half an hour later by a seventh, delayed by a breakdown in the catapult gear on the cruiser Tone.

On Midway Captain Simard was alerted in time and put up all his planes, but his 26 fighters were no match for the Japanese Zeros, which knocked out 17 of them and crippled seven others to such an extent that they had to be written off. The Japanese lost only six. The Midway air force was not silenced for all that. Lieutenant Joichi Tomonaga, who led the first wave, signalled back to Nagumo that in his opinion a second attack was necessary.

The Japanese Admiral acted on Tomonaga's report and ordered that the torpedo-carrying bombers of the second wave (108 planes), armed to attack any U.S. ships that might appear, should have their torpedoes replaced by bombs, and the dive-bombers their armour-piercing bombs by high-explosive ones. This decision seemed justified by the ferocity of the Midway air force's counter-attack. It is true that Captain Simard's pilots pressed their charges home, as the saying was in the days of cavalry; it is also true that the training of the men on the one side and the efficiency of the machines on the other were unequal to the courage displayed. Thirty-nine torpedo-carrying aircraft and dive-bombers had attacked the Japanese without causing any damage to their ships; 17 of these planes had been shot down and seven were declared beyond repair on their return. A squadron of Flying Fortresses then bombed the enemy convoy from a height of 21,000 feet, also without success. Though these attacks had been fruitless, Admiral Nagumo nevertheless threw in his second wave of fighters.

Bombs or torpedoes? Meanwhile, at 0728 hours, Tone's seaplane signalled that it had spotted ten enemy ships 240 miles away, steaming south-south-east. Not until 0820 hours did the pilot see, and then only vaguely, that there was an aircraft-carrier with them. Though this report was far from clear, it put Nagumo in a very embarrassing position. If he sent up his second wave

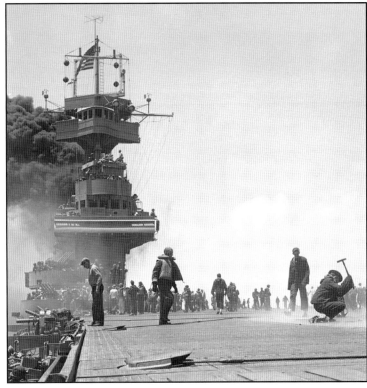

Crewmembers of the USS Yortown work hard to repair the damage.

dive-bombers (36 planes) to attack this formation, they would be without fighter escort and would take a heavy beating. The same danger faced Akagi's and Kaga's torpedo-bombers, which were now loaded with bombs instead of torpedoes. These were less likely to be successful against warships. If he waited for the first wave to land on his carriers when they returned from Midway he would then be able to attack with all his forces. And so at 0855 hours Nagumo signalled his squadron: "After landing, formation will proceed north provisionally. We expect to make contact with the enemy and destroy him."

Whereupon the armourers of the aircraft-carriers again threw themselves into the task of changing the weapons on the aircraft, replacing H.E. bombs with torpedoes and armour-piercing bombs. As time was short, they piled up the bombs alongside the aircraft in the hangars.

A change of fortune

At 0552 hours on June 4 a message to Admirals Fletcher and Spruance announced that the enemy forces with four aircraft-carriers were 230 miles to their south-west. Fletcher, the senior of the two officers and therefore in command of the whole force, gave the order to attack. From 0702 hours Task Force 16, now sailing towards the enemy, sent up 116 planes. Yorktown, in Task Force 17, waited until 0838 hours before launching her 35.

It has been said that Rear-Admiral Spruance had calculated the time so as to surprise the enemy aircraft-carriers just when their flight-decks would be cluttered up with planes returning from Midway. With admirable, almost unprecedented modesty he himself has denied the flattering legend in his preface to Commanders Fuchida's and Okumiya's book, Midway.

"When I read the account of the events of June 4, 1942 I am struck once more by the part played by chance in warfare. The authors congratulate us on having chosen the moment of our attack on the Japanese aircraft-carriers when they were at their most vulnerable, that is with their flight-decks encumbered with planes ready to take off. We did not choose this moment deliberately. For my part I had only the feeling that we had to achieve surprise and strike the enemy planes with all the strength at our command as soon as we met them."

The first U.S. Navy squadron to attack, 15 TBD Devastator torpedo-bombers under Lieutenant-Commander John Waldron, from Hornet, appeared at about 0930, skimming over the tops of the waves. A few minutes later they had all been shot down and only one out of their total crew of 30 survived. They were slow and vulnerable to enemy fire. Fuchida and Okumiya described this unsuccessful but heroic attack in the following words:

"The first enemy carrier planes to attack were 15 torpedo bombers. When first spotted by our screening ships and combat air patrol, they were still not visible from the carriers, but they soon appeared as tiny dark specks in the sky, a little above the horizon, on Akagi's starboard bow. The distant wings flashed in the sun. Occasionally one of the specks burst into a spark of flame and trailed black smoke as it fell into the water. Our fighters were on the job, and the enemy again seemed to be without fighter protection.

"Presently a report came in from a Zero group leader: 'All 15 enemy torpedo bombers shot down.' Nearly 50 Zeros had gone to intercept the unprotected enemy formation! Small wonder that it did not get through."

The squadrons of Devastator torpedo-bombers from Enterprise and Yorktown were almost as unfortunate: they lost 20 out of 26 planes to the Japanese fighters and A.A. guns. Worse still, not a single one of their torpedoes reached its target. So by 1015 hours Nagumo was winning. At the cost of six of his own planes he had destroyed 83 of his enemy's and at 1030 hours he would unleash on the American squadron a wave of 102 planes, including 54 torpedo-bombers and 36 dive-bombers. He was confident that they would destroy the Americans.

By 1028 hours, however, the Rising Sun had been decisively defeated.

The American planes had encountered difficulties during their approach, as the position they had been given was erroneous, the Japanese ships having changed direction. This caused an unwelcome detour. Some Wildcat fighter squadrons lost the torpedo-carrying aircraft they were supposed to be escorting. The massacre described above was the result. But the heroic sacrifice of Waldron and his men paid off a few minutes later. The Zero fighters were so busy tracking down Waldron's planes at low level that they were too late to prevent an attack by Douglas SBD Dauntlesses, which dive-bombed the Japanese aircraft-carriers from a height of nearly 20,000 feet. On the carriers themselves, the Japanese were too busy warding off torpedoes to see the second attack.

The scene has been described by an eyewitness on the flight-deck of the ill-fated Akagi:

"I looked up to see three black enemy planes plummeting towards our ship. Some of our machine guns managed to fire a few frantic bursts at them, but it was too late. The plump silhouettes of the American 'Dauntless' dive-bombers grew larger, and then a number of black objects suddenly floated eerily from their wings. Bombs! Down they came straight towards me! I fell intuitively to the deck and crawled behind a command post mantlet.

"The terrifying scream of the dive bombers reached me first, followed by the crashing explosion of a direct hit. There was a blinding flash and then a second explosion, much louder than the first. I was shaken by a weird blast of warm air. There was still another shock, but less severe, apparently a near-miss. Then followed a startling quiet as the barking of guns suddenly ceased. I got up and looked at the sky. The enemy planes were already gone from sight …

"Looking about, I was horrified at the destruction that had been wrought in a matter of seconds. There was a huge hole in the flight deck just behind the amidships elevator. The elevator itself, twisted like molten glass, was drooping into the hangar. Deck plates reeled upwards in grotesque configurations. Planes stood tail up, belching livid flame and jet black smoke. Reluctant tears streamed down my cheeks as I watched the fires spread."

A Hiryu escaped the first shattering dive-bomber attack which knocked out Kaga, Akagi, and Soryu — but not for long. Here her blazing and abandoned hulk wallows sluggishly in a calm sea. She finally sank around 0915 on June 5.

Nagumo's force destroyed

The end of the battle of Midway was swift. The Akagi was racked by explosions as her petrol and piles of bombs went up, causing widespread fires and destruction. Akagi's radio was out of action, and Vice-Admiral Nagumo and his staff left the ship at 1046 hours.

"As the number of dead and wounded increased and the fires got further out of control, Captain Aoki finally decided at 1800 that the ship must be abandoned. The injured were lowered into boats and cutters sent alongside by the screening destroyers. Many uninjured men leapt into the sea and swam away from the stricken ship. Destroyers Arashi and Nowaki picked up all survivors. When the rescue work was complete, Captain Aoki radioed to Admiral Nagumo at 1920 from one of the destroyers, asking permission to sink the crippled carrier. This inquiry was monitored by the combined fleet flagship, whence Admiral Yamamoto dispatched an order at 2225 to delay the carrier's disposition. Upon receipt of this instruction, the captain returned to his carrier alone. He reached the anchor deck, which was still free from fire, and there lashed himself to an anchor..."

A few miles away, Kaga, hit by four bombs, had also become a raging inferno and her crew were attempting to control the flames amidst explosions which were causing widespread death and destruction. The ship had been attacked by Enterprise's and Hornet's dive-bombers which were under the command of Lieutenant-Commander Clarence W. McClusky. Soryu was bombed by planes led by Lieutenant-Commander Maxwell Leslie and by formations from Yorktown. By 1040 hours Soryu's rudder and engines were out of action and her crew was surrounded by fires and explosions.

The only unit of the Japanese Carrier Striking Force now fit to fight was Hiryu. In accordance with Nagumo's order she sent off some 40 planes in two waves to attack Task Force 17. At mid-day, 18 dive-bombers appeared above Yorktown. The Americans had been warned in time by radar, and the A.A. wiped out 12 planes, but two bombs reached their target and the powerful vessel was brought to a standstill at 1220 hours. She had got under way but Hiryu's aircraft attacked again through a seemingly impenetrable barrage of fire and scored hits with two torpedoes. Seeing his

ship in danger of capsizing, her commander ordered her to be abandoned and taken in tow. This was to be Hiryu's last action. Only 15 of her planes, including six fighters, returned. At 1630 hours, Spruance sighted her and sent in 24 Dauntlesses under McClusky. The Japanese vessel whipped her speed up to 33 knots, but she was hit by four bombs at 1700 hours. All the planes on the flight deck were set on fire and all means of escape from the ship were cut off. At dusk Task Force 16 set course eastwards as Spruance did not care to risk a night battle with an enemy force containing the battleships Haruna and Kirishima, against which he was clearly at a disadvantage.

Between 1900 and 1930 hours, Soryu and Kaga both disappeared beneath the waters of the Pacific. In the morning of the following day Nagumo, with the authority of Admiral Yamamoto, finished off the wrecks of Akagi and Hiryu with torpedoes. The commander of the second, Rear-Admiral Tamon Yamaguchi, obstinately refused to leave his ship and, to ensure that he went down with her, tied himself to the bridge.

Yamamoto gives up

On board Yamato, the Commander-in-Chief of the Combined Fleet could do no more than admit his powerlessness to redeem the situation now that his various detachments were so widely scattered. After a series of orders and counter-orders, on June 5 he finally confirmed the abandonment of operations against Midway and the return to their bases of his several detachments.

This was not to be done without further loss, however. In the 7th Cruiser Division, Mogami was in collision during the night with Mikuma. Hounded by enemy planes in the daylight, the former was further damaged and put out of action for a year. The latter went down at about noon on June 6. A few hours later the Japanese submarine I-168 (Lieutenant-Commander Yahachi Tanabe), which had shelled Midway on the night of June 4–5, surprised Yorktown as she was being towed slowly back to Pearl Harbor. Manoeuvring swiftly and decisively it sank her with two torpedoes and cut the destroyer Hammann in half with a third.

This was the end of one of the most decisive battles of World War II, the effects of which were felt far beyond the waters of the Pacific. It deprived Japan of her freedom of action and it allowed the two Anglo-Saxon powers to go ahead with their policy of "Germany first", as agreed between Churchill and Roosevelt.

The Americans had lost 307 dead and 147 planes. The Japanese lost 4 fleet carriers, 332 planes and 3,500 dead, and these heavy losses included the cream of her naval air forces. The results show that, though they had been dealt a worse hand than the enemy, Nimitz, Fletcher, and Spruance had played their cards better than Yamamoto and Nagumo. Chance had played her part too, though. What would have happened if Tone's seaplane had not been half an hour late in taking off? We shall never know.

On June 6–7 the Japanese occupied the undefended islands of Kiska and Attu in the Aleutians.

Admiral Isoroku Yamamoto, C in C of Japanese Navy.

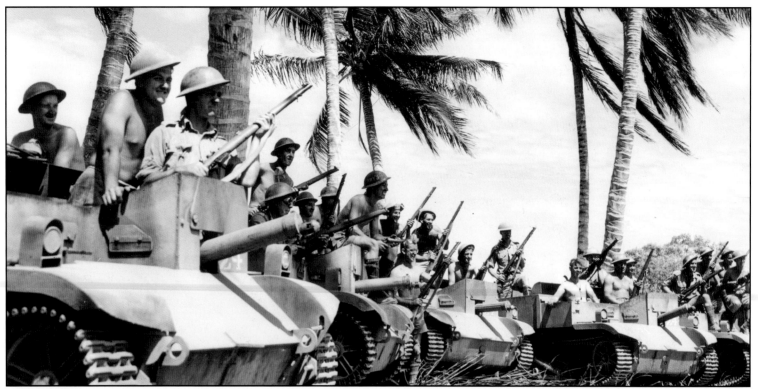

Port Moresby - Australian Universal Carrier, MG, with vickers .303in machine gun.

At the beginning of March 1942 Japanese bombs were falling on the eastern half of New Guinea, the great jungle-covered island off the northern coast of Australia. The bombers came from Rabaul on the island of New Britain, to the east.

Rabaul, the capital of territory mandated to Australia at the end of World War I, which included the Bismarcks and a strip along the northern coast of New Guinea, had been captured on January 23 by the Japanese Army's 5,000man South Seas Detachment (Major-General Tomitaro Horii) supported by the Navy's 4th Fleet (Vice-Admiral Shigeyoshi Inouye). Sailing into its spacious harbour, ringed by smoking volcanoes, the invaders in a few hours forced the small Australian garrison to scatter into the hills.

The Japanese found Rabaul "a nice little town", with wide-eaved bungalows surrounded by red hibiscus. General Horii, the conqueror of Guam, rounded up the white civilians and sent them off to Japan in the transport Montevideo Maru (they were all lost en route when the ship was sunk by an American submarine). Then he began building an air base. Admiral Inouye helped to make the base secure by occupying Kavieng on New Ireland to the north. To the south-east, bombing took care of Bougainville, northernmost of the long string of Solomon Islands.

The towns of Lae and Salamaua, in the Huon Gulf in the east of New Guinea, had been heavily bombed in the preliminary attack on Rabaul on January 21. The civilians fled, some on foot to the wild interior, some in native canoes down the Solomon Sea, hugging the New Guinea coast. One party, after a voyage of about two weeks, put in at Gona, an Anglican mission on the coast in Australia's own Territory of Papua, in the south-east of New Guinea.

The arrival of the refugees from the Mandated Territory was long remembered by Father James Benson, the priest at Gona. The big sailing canoes against a flaming sunset sky brought through the surf "thirty-two woefully weatherbeaten refugees whose poor sun- and salt-cracked lips and bearded faces bore evidence of a fortnight's constant exposure." With only the clothes they fled in, "they looked indeed a sorry lot of ragamuffins". Next morning they began the five-day walk to Kokoda, a government station about 50 miles inland. From there planes could take them to Port Moresby, the territorial capital on the Coral Sea, facing Australia.

Planes flying from Kokoda to Port Moresby had to skim the green peaks of the Owen Stanley Range, the towering, jungle-covered mountain chain that runs the length of the Papuan peninsula. After a flight of about 45 minutes they put down at a dusty airstrip in bare brown foothills. From the foothills a road descended to Port Moresby, in peacetime a sleepy copra port with tin-roofed warehouses baking in the tropical sun along the waterfront. A single jetty extended into a big harbour; beyond, a channel led to a second harbour large enough to have sheltered the Australian fleet in World War I.

Because of its fine harbour and its position dominating the populous east coast of Australia, Port Moresby was heavily ringed on military maps in Tokyo. On orders from Imperial General Headquarters the first air raid was launched from Rabaul on February 3. The bombers did a thorough job and returned unscathed. Port Moresby's handful of obsolete planes and small anti-aircraft guns was no match for modern Japanese aircraft.

Star of the Japanese air fleet was the Mitsubishi A6M Zero fighter-bomber, one of the best planes of the war. Armed with two 20-mm cannon and two 7.7-mm machine guns, it could carry 264 pounds of bombs and was fast and agile. Its range of 1,150 miles and ceiling of 32,800 feet also made it invaluable for reconnaissance.

To facilitate the bombing of Port Moresby, some 550 miles from Rabaul, Tokyo ordered General Horii to occupy Lae and Salamaua, Lae to be used as an advanced air base, Salamaua to secure Lae. At 0100 hours on the morning of March 8 a battalion of Horii's 144th Regiment made an unopposed landing at Salamaua — the first Japanese landing on New Guinea. An hour later Inouye's Maizuru 2nd Special Naval Landing Force (S.N.L.F.) marines occupied Lae. The naval force, which included engineers and a base unit, then took over at Salamaua. Horii's infantrymen returned to Rabaul to await orders for the next move in the south-west Pacific.

Operation "MO"

On May 2, while the South Seas Detachment was boarding its transports, a force left Rabaul harbour for the small island of Tagula in the southern Solomons to establish a seaplane base in support of Operation "MO". It landed without opposition the following day, and a few days later put a construction unit ashore on the large island of Guadalcanal to build an airfield.

The Port Moresby invasion force steamed south from Rabaul on May 4 in five transports, well escorted. Off Bougainville the convoy was joined by the light carrier Shoho, with six cruisers. Two fleet carriers, Shokaku and Zuikaku, stood by south of the Solomons. As the invasion convoy was nearing the eastern point of New Guinea on May 7, the carrier Shoho, in the lead, was attacked by U.S. carrier planes and sunk, along with a cruiser. Admiral Inouye then ordered the transports back to Rabaul.

The following day the Battle of the Coral Sea was fought between the U.S. carriers Lexington and Yorktown and the Japanese Shokaku and Zuikaku — the first carrier battle in history. One Japanese carrier was damaged, the other lost most of her planes. The Lexington was sunk. The battle was therefore not a clear-cut victory for either side; but the invasion of Port Moresby had been blocked. For this, credit was due to the U.S. Navy cryptanalysts in Hawaii who had cracked the Japanese fleet code and thus enabled the Allies to intercept the convoy.

Operation "MO" was not abandoned, only postponed; and the release of Japanese forces from the Philippines after the surrender of Bataan and Corregidor on May 6 made an expanded operation possible, with the Yazawa and Aoba Detachments at Davao and the Kawaguchi Detachment at Palau added to the South Seas Detachment, all to come under the 17th Army (Lieutenant-General Harukichi Hyakutake), which was established on May 18.

In Tokyo, euphoria was at its height. At Army headquarters in late May, Seizo Okada, a war correspondent assigned to the South Seas Detachment, had to fight his way through a crowd of "provincials" (Japanese Army slang for civilians) clamouring for permission to go abroad with the Army. After receiving his credentials from a major, Okada asked for a pair of army boots. "Behind a screen that stood by the Major some staff officers were talking and puffing at cigarettes. One of them, as plump as a pig, broke in, 'Hey, what are you talking about? Boots? Don't worry about your boots. You'll get lots of beautiful ones out there — damned beautiful enemy boots'.

"The mocking words drove the other officers into a fit of boisterous laughter. They too, like myself or any other Japanese, were puffed up like toy balloons by the 'brilliant initial success' of the Pacific War."

A week later came news of the first crushing setback. At Midway on June 7 the Japanese Navy was decisively defeated by the U.S. fleet, with a heavy loss of carriers.

Plans for operations in the southern Pacific had to be revised. Assaults against New Caledonia, Fiji, and Samoa were postponed indefinitely; and, for lack of carriers, Operation "MO" was changed from an amphibious assault to a land attack on Port Moresby over the Owen Stanley mountains, to be made by the South Seas Detachment with the help of the 15th Independent Engineer Regiment (Colonel Yosuke Yokoyama).

An advance echelon under Colonel Yokoyama, consisting of the engineers, a battalion of Horii's 144th Infantry Regiment, a company of marines of the Sasebo 5th S.N.L.F., and some

Kokoda trail - Australian troops march through mud.

artillery, anti-aircraft, and service units, in all about 1,800 men, was to land between Gona and Buna, an Australian government station about ten miles down the coast, advance inland to capture Kokoda, and prepare they way for Horii's main force to cross the Owen Stanley Range. Reconnaissance Zeros had spotted a red ribbon of earth winding over the mountains and assumed it to be a road. The engineers were to put it into shape to take trucks, if possible, or at least pack horses.

While the Yokoyama Force was embarking in Rabaul harbour, General Hyakutake on July 18 prepared a plan to assist Horii with a flanking seaplane attack based on Samarai at the entrance to Milne Bay, the 20-mile long, 7-mile wide bay at the eastern end of New Guinea. The Navy was to seize Samarai on August 25 with the help of a battalion of the Kawaguchi Detachment. In this latest version of Operation "MO", the Yazawa Detachment, consisting mainly of the 41st Infantry Regiment (Colonel Kiyomi Yazawa), was allocated to Horii.

Advance to Kokoda

Late on the afternoon of July 21, the Yokoyama Force, in three heavily-escorted transports, began landing on the New Guinea coast just east of Gona. Allied planes arrived and damaged two transports, but only 40 men were lost, and there was no other opposition. At Gona the missionaries had fled, and Buna was found to be deserted when the marines arrived next day to start building an airfield. Colonel Yokoyama concentrated his army troops at a point about half-way between Gona and Buna, where a corduroy road led inland for about 15 miles.

On the evening of the landing the infantry battalion (Lieutenant-Colonel Hatsuo Tsukamoto) and a company of engineers began the march inland, about 900 men with torches, some on bicycles, with orders to "push on night and day to the line of the mountain range".

Half-way to Kokoda they were fired upon by a few Australian and native soldiers, but these were easily dispersed. The natives melted away into the jungle. The Australians, part of a company of raw militiamen, tried to stop the invaders by destroying the bridge that carried the road over the Kumusi river, but when the Japanese threw up a bridge and pressed on, they retreated. On the night of July 28, in a thick mist, Tsukamoto bombarded Kokoda with mortars and a mountain gun and drove the defenders out.

The Japanese were puzzled by the weakness of the opposition. They did not know that the Allies, after recovering from the surprise of the landing, had persuaded themselves that the object of the landing was only to establish airfields in the Buna area. The Australians found it impossible to believe that the Japanese would attempt an overland attack on Port Moresby. The "road" over the mountains was only a native footpath, two or three feet wide.

Known as the Kokoda Track, the path crossed a range of mountains described graphically by an Australian who had made the crossing on foot: "Imagine an area of approximately one hundred miles long. Crumple and fold this into a series of ridges, each rising higher and higher until 7,000 feet is reached, then declining in ridges of 3,000 feet. Cover this thickly with jungle, short trees and tall trees, tangled with great, entwining savage vines." The days were hot and humid, the nights cold; frequent afternoon rains made the track "a treacherous mass of moving mud".

By August 21, when the main Japanese force got ashore under cover of a storm, Horii had landed on the New Guinea coast a total of 8,000 Army troops, 3,000 naval construction troops, and some 450 marines of the Sasebo 5th S.N.L.F. At the head of a formidable body of fighting troops he rode into Kokoda astride his white horse on August 24.

He found that Colonel Tsukamoto's infantry had already pushed up the Kokoda Track for several miles and taken the next village, Deniki, from which the Australian militiamen, evidently reinforced, had been trying to retake Kokoda. Defeated at Deniki, they had withdrawn up a steep slope to Isurava. This was to be Horii's first objective. He began shelling it on August 26.

Disaster in Milne Bay

Bad luck dogged the Milne Bay operation from the start. The second week in August, the battalion of the Kawaguchi Detachment assigned to the 8th Fleet (Vice-Admiral Gunichi Mikawa) for the operation was sent instead to help clear Guadalcanal in the Solomons, where U.S. Marines had landed on August 7. A replacement battalion could not arrive in time. Admiral Mikawa, who had won a brilliant naval victory at Guadalcanal on August 9, would have no help from the Army at Milne Bay.

Milne Bay - Curliss Killyhawk of RAAF - Truscott returns from operations - on PSP matting.

At the last minute the target was changed. Reports from reconnaissance planes in mid-August that the Allies were building an airfield at the head of Milne Bay near Gili Gili led planners to change the landing from Samarai, at the mouth of the bay, to Gili Gili.

The Japanese knew little about the Gili Gili area, in peace-time the site of a coconut plantation. Low-lying rain clouds usually protected it from reconnaissance. Estimating that it was held by not more than three infantry companies and 30 aircraft, Mikawa allotted only about 1,500 men to the invasion. Most of them were to come from Kavieng: 612 marines of the Kure 5th S.N.L.F.

(Commander Shojiro Hayashi), 362 16th Naval Pioneer Unit troops, and 197 marines of the Sasebo 5th S.N.L.F. The Kavieng convoys were to sail up Milne Bay and land at Rabi, about three miles east of the Gili Gili jetty. At the same time, 353 marines of the Sasebo 5th S.N.L.F. at Buna, carried in seven big, wooden, motor-driven barges, were to land at Taupota on the Solomon Sea side and march over the mountains to Gili Gili.

The overland force was the first casualty of the operation. As it chugged down the coast under cloud cover on August 24 it was sighted and reported by a "coastwatcher" — one of the Australian organisation of planters and officials who had taken to the hills with wireless sets. The following day the marines beached the barges on Goodenough Island and went ashore to eat lunch. At

Jungle village area where Jap & Australian forces are engaged.

that moment the clouds parted and 12 Australian P-40 fighter planes swooped low and destroyed the barges. The Buna marines were left stranded.

Two cruiser-escorted transports with Commander Hayashi and the first echelon of the Kavieng marines arrived safely at the head of Milne Bay in a downpour on the night of August 25. Shortly before midnight Hayashi began the landings at a point he believed to be Rabi. But he had no reliable map, and in the darkness and rain he landed about seven miles to the east on a swampy coastal shelf where the mountains came down almost to the water. His only means of advance westward toward Gili Gili was a muddy 12-foot track.

Hayashi was a stickler for night operations. He waited until darkness fell on August 26 to attack his first objective, a plantation astride the track at K. B. Mission, lightly held by Australian militia. Preceded by a flame-thrower, his troops tried to outflank the defenders by wading into the bay on one side and the swamp on the other. By dawn they had almost succeeded; but at first light they retired into the jungle.

The following night the attack was resumed in greater force, the second echelon from Kavieng having arrived. This time the Japanese used two small tanks-the first tanks to be landed on the New Guinea coast. They each had a strong headlight which, shining through the rain, enabled them to illuminate the Australian positions while the attackers remained in darkness.

With the help of the tanks, Hayashi's men cleared K. B. Mission, crossed the Gama river beyond, and before dawn on August 28 were attacking an airstrip that U.S. engineers were building between Rabi and Gili Gili. There, lacking the tanks, which had bogged down in mud and had had to be abandoned, they were stopped by heavy fire. At daylight they withdrew into the jungle.

Commander Hayashi had already asked Admiral Mikawa to send him reinforcements. He had been deprived of his overland force and had lost a considerable part of his food and ammunition when Allied aircraft sank the steel barges ferrying it ashore. He had met ground opposition greater than he expected and found the terrain worse than anything he could have imagined. Reinforcements landed on the night of August 29 under cover of a heavy mist. They were 568 marines of the Kure 3rd S.N.L.F. and 200 of the Yokosuka 5th S.N.L.F., all under Commander Minoro Yano who, being senior to Hayashi, took command of operations.

Before one o'clock on the morning of August 31 the combined Japanese forces launched a furious assault on the airstrip. They were beaten back by intense fire from anti-tank guns, heavy machine guns, and mortars, expertly sited with a clear field of fire and backed by heavy artillery positioned in the rear. Before day broke, three Japanese bugle calls rang out, the signal for retreat.

The Australians pursued. By nightfall on September 1 they had retaken K. B. Mission. Commander Yano, setting up defences on the track to block the pursuit, cabled Admiral Mikawa on September 3 for permission to withdraw from Milne Bay. He himself had been wounded; Hayashi had been killed; he had lost 600 men and had more than 300 wounded on his hands. The rest of the men, most of them suffering from trench foot, jungle rot, and tropical fevers, could not hold out. Mikawa sanctioned the evacuation. By dawn of September 6, Japanese ships, carrying the 1,300 men remaining of the 1,900-man invasion force, were on their way to Rabaul.

The crowning misfortune of the Milne Bay invasion was the miscalculation of the strength of the defenders. Unknown to the Japanese, the Allies had landed at the head of Milne Bay between June 25 and August 20 some 4,500 Australian infantrymen, supported by about 3,000 Australian and 1,300 American engineer, artillery, and service units.

Japanese fanaticism had met its match; but it had been a close run thing.

The Japanese retreat

On September 20 General Horii called together his commanders and praised them for their success in crossing "the so-called impregnable Stanley Range". At the proper time they were "to strike a crushing blow at the enemy's positions at Port Moresby". The halt at Ioribaiwa would give the tired troops, many of them wounded and ill, a chance to regain their fighting strength. Most were hungry; little or no rice remained in the dumps. Horii had already ordered detachments to dig up native gardens in the area and sent parties over the mountains to bring up provisions from the rear. To block an Australian attack, he ordered his engineers to build a stockade of tree trunks.

The Australians did not attack; but no supplies came from the rear, no Zeros flew over. "An atmosphere of uneasiness," noted Okada, "stole over the mountain, a feeling that things were not going well at Guadalcanal. On September 24 in a night of drizzling rain the blow fell. A signal commander came into Horii's tent with a message from Imperial General Headquarters ordering Horii to withdraw his force from the Owen Stanleys to the coast at Buna."

The reason for the order was a major defeat at Guadalcanal on September 15, in which the Kawaguchi Detachment had been virtually wiped out. Imperial General Headquarters decided to subordinate everything to the retaking of Guadalcanal. Once that had been accomplished, it would be possible to resume Operation "MO". In the meantime, Horii's mission was to defend the Buna beach-head.

For Horii, the order "to abandon this position after all the blood the soldiers have shed and the hardships they have endured" was agonising. He sent his chief-of-staff, Lieutenant-Colonel Toyanari Tanaka, to break the news to the battalion commanders. Some of them almost rebelled, urging a desperate, single-handed thrust into Port Moresby.

On September 25 the movement back over the mountains began. The order to withdraw had crushed the spirit of the soldiers, which, Okada reported, "had been kept up through sheer pride". For a time they remained stupefied. "Then they began to move, and once in retreat they fled for dear life. None of them had ever thought that a Japanese soldier would turn his back on the enemy. But they were actually beating a retreat!"

As soon as they accepted this bitter fact, "they were seized by an instinctive desire to live". Each tried to flee faster than his comrades. Passing by bodies of men killed in the fighting of early September, already rotting and covered with maggots, the soldiers stopped only to dig for taroes or yams. They found little; the fields had been dug up almost inch by inch. By the time they reached the crest of the Range, they were fleeing from starvation, a greater menace than the Allied planes roaring overhead or enemy guns rumbling in the rear.

To delay the Australian pursuit, which began on September 27, Horii ordered a rearguard battalion to make a stand on the heights above Eora Creek. There it was attacked by troops of the Australian 16th Brigade on October 21. Reinforced from Kokoda and Buna, it held out for seven days, long enough for Horii to evacuate Kokoda and set up his last defences, at Oivi and Gorari in the foothills between Kokoda and the Kumusi river.

At Oivi, strongly fortified by Colonel Yazawa, the Australians attacking on November 5 could make no headway; but at Gorari, where Colonel Tsukamoto was in command (Colonel Kusunose having been evacuated because of sickness and wounds), an Australian assault on November 10 succeeded, after heavy fighting. Yazawa's position was now untenable. He withdrew his 900-man force after dark that evening over a little-known track leading north-east to the mouth of the Kumusi. With him was General Horii, who had been on an inspection trip to Oivi.

The rest of the South Seas Detachment, about 1,200 men, began crossing the Kumusi river on the night of November 12, guided by the light of a bonfire. They had no bridge. Incendiary bombs dropped from Allied planes had burned the wooden bridge built in August by the Yokoyama Force and defeated all attempts to replace it. The soldiers crossed in six-man folding boats, then pushed on in the darkness toward Buna.

Seizo Okada crossed with the vanguard. Stopping at a newsmen's hut about halfway to Buna, he watched the "men of the mountains" as they moved along the road, day and night, toward the coast. "They had shaggy hair and beards. Their uniforms were soiled with blood and mud and sweat, and torn to pieces. There were infantrymen without rifles, men walking on bare feet, men wearing blankets or straw rice-bags instead of uniforms, men reduced to skin and bone plodding along with the help of a stick, men gasping and crawling on the ground."

The stretcher-bearers, themselves too weak to carry stretchers, dragged the sick and wounded to the overcrowded field hospital near Buna and laid them on straw mats in the jungle. "The soldiers had eaten anything to appease hunger — young shoots of trees, roots of grass, even cakes of earth. These things had injured their stomachs so badly that when they were brought back to the field hospital they could no longer digest any food. Many of them vomited blood and died."

Later, Okada learned that General Horii had drowned while on the march northwards with Yazawa. Horii, anxious to rejoin his men at Buna, tried to cross the lower Kumusi river on a log raft. In the swift current the raft carrying him and Colonel Tanaka overturned.

So ended, in tragedy, the overland march on Port Moresby. Misgivings about it had been felt by at least one officer at Imperial General Headquarters, Colonel Masanobu Tsuji, who warned, "Cross the mountains and you will get the worst of it." At the end

Australian & US troops inspect knocked out Japanese tanks.

his verdict was, "a blunder".

Though the Buna beach-head was reinforced from Rabaul and held out for several months, Operation "MO" was never resumed. Beginning early in October, the attention of Imperial General Headquarters was diverted from New Guinea and focused on Guadalcanal.

US Marines wade up Tenaru River led by native guides.

Allied resources in the Pacific were stretched to the limit in the summer of 1942, and the greater part of the American war effort was directed toward the European theatre and the defeat of Germany. The Japanese, checked only by the crucial naval Battle of Midway in June 1942, were riding a tide of victory and easy conquests. Tulagi Island, site of the headquarters of the British Solomon Islands Protectorate, was not on the original schedule of targets the Japanese had projected for the South Pacific, but it too was taken as the victory tide swept onward. The seaplane base and radio station that the Japanese had established on Tulagi did not particularly worry the Allies, but reports in June 1942 that Japanese troops had begun levelling an aircraft runway

on the kunai grass plains of the Lunga river on the large island of Guadalcanal, 20 miles south across Sealark Channel from Tulagi, were a different story. Here was a clear threat to the shipping lifeline stretched across the South Pacific from the U.S. to New Zealand and Australia.

At the time the Japanese moved to Tagula, the nearest American troops were on the outposts of Espiritu Santo in the New Hebrides, 550 miles away. An airfield was rushed to completion there, to be ready by the end of July to support operations against the Japanese. The American Joint Chiefs-of-Staff, urged on by the Navy's leader, Admiral Ernest J. King, had decided to mount a ground offensive to halt the enemy drive to the south and to provide a base for offensive operations against

Rabaul, the Japanese area headquarters and nerve centre on New Britain in the Bismarcks.

Guadalcanal and Tulagi were the objectives, and the assault force was the only amphibious trained division readily available, the 1st Marine Division. It was, in fact, the only unit of its size that was available. Commanded by Major-General Alexander A. Vandegrift, a veteran of the jungle fighting of the Banana Wars in the Caribbean, the 1st Division had been formed in 1940 and included many veteran Marines in its ranks as well as a number of men without combat or expeditionary experience. Its forward echelon had just arrived in Wellington, New Zealand, for six months of intensive combat training when the word was passed that it would go into battle instead. Some troops were still at sea; one of its regiments, the 7th Marines, was committed to the defence of Samoa and the 2nd Marines of the 2nd Marine Division had to be sent out from San Diego to replace it. Other major elements to be attached to the 1st Division were located on New Caledonia and in the Hawaiian Islands. All had to be alerted, equipped, and assembled in less than a month's time to meet a D-day of August 7, 1942.

Working around the clock and pushing aside New Zealand dock workers who wanted to invoke union labour rules, the Marines in Wellington unloaded transports as fast as they arrived, sorted and repacked equipment and supplies for combat, and loaded ship again. There was not enough room for all the division's motor transport and most of the heavier trucks had to be left behind. Only 60 days of supplies and rations, ammunition for 10 days' heavy fighting (units of fire), and the bare minimum of individual equipment were taken.

Constant air attack

Almost constant Japanese air attacks, which began on the afternoon of August 7, thoroughly disrupted unloading as the transports and escorts manoeuvred to escape the rain of bombs. The Marines did not have enough shore party troops to handle the supplies that did reach the beach. Ships' captains in a hurry to empty their holds and inexperienced coxswains combined forces to dump an unprogrammed jumble of ammunition, rations, tentage, vehicles, and assorted supplies on the shoreline, offering another tempting target for the Japanese planes. When Turner reluctantly sailed south to Espiritu Santo and New Caledonia, only 37 days' supply of rations and four units of fire had been landed. Vandegrift had 16,000 men ashore, 6,000 on Tulagi, with the rest still on board ship when the task force departed.

After this event, the commanding general of Army forces in the South Pacific, Major-General Millard F. Harmon, was far from optimistic about the chances of success for the Guadalcanal venture. On August 11 he wrote to the Army's Chief-of-Staff in Washington, General George C. Marshall:

"The thing that impresses me more than anything else in connection with the Solomon action is that we are not prepared to follow up … We have seized a strategic position from which future operations in the Bismarcks can be strongly supported. Can the Marines hold it? There is considerable room for doubt."

Cast loose, or at least promised only a tenuous lifeline to Allied support bases, the 1st Marine Division made do with

Henderson field - ground crew load 500lb bombs for Grumman TBF Avenger - on PSP matting.

what it had. The completion of the airfield that the Japanese had begun was crucial; without it there was little ground for hope that the Marines could stay on Guadalcanal. Japanese engineering equipment was used to the fullest extent; captured Japanese weapons were included in defensive positions; Japanese rations were added to the Marines' meagre stocks; and Japanese trucks were used to supplement the small American motor pool. The airfield was ready for use on August 18; it was named Henderson Field after a Marine pilot killed in the Battle of Midway. On the day that the runway was finished, the Japanese took their

first step toward wresting control of the island back from the Americans, landing a battalion of the 28th Regiment to the east of Vandegrift's perimeter. This was to be the first of many runs by the "Tokyo Express," a cruiser–destroyer transport force commanded by Rear-Admiral Raizo Tanaka, which was largely responsible for the reinforcement and resupply of the Japanese on Guadalcanal.

The red letter day for the Marines was August 20. Two squadrons flew in to Henderson Field from the escort carrier Long Island, 19 Grumman F4F Wildcat fighters from Marine Fighting Squadron 223 and 12 Douglas SBD-3 Dauntless dive-bombers from Marine Scout-Bomber Squadron 232. The planes came just in time to help with the destruction of the Japanese battalion that had landed two days before. Making a night attack headlong against the positions of the 1st Marines' battalion holding the west bank of the Ilu River, which marked the eastern edge of Vandegrift's perimeter, the Japanese were ground up in a fury of artillery, machine gun, and 37-mm canister fire. When daylight came, a Marine battalion mopped up the remnants of the attacking force, helped by strafing attacks by the newly arrived Wildcats. The Japanese commander, Colonel Kiyono Ichiki, disheartened by his failure, committed suicide; 800 of his men had died in the fighting.

Colonel Ichiki, like his superior in Rabaul, Lieutenant-General Harukichi Hyakutake, commanding the 17th Army, had underestimated both the strength and the determination of the Marines to hold out. Time and again, the Japanese were to repeat Ichiki's error, sending thousands of men from Rabaul but never enough at one time so that Vandegrift could not handle them. The troops available to Hyakutake in August and September was more than enough to overwhelm the Marine defences, but these troops were never committed in sufficient force to sustain a determined attack.

US Marines - corporal inspect Japanese souvenirs.

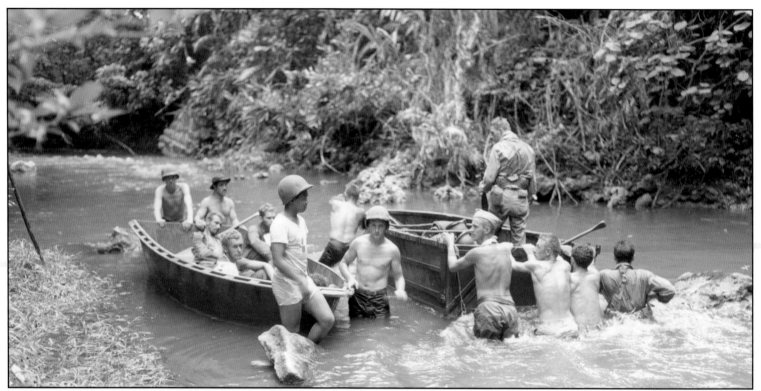

Matanikan River boats deliver supplies & evacuates wounded.

General Vandegrift never lost sight of his primary mission of defending Henderson Field. He was aggressive and mounted a number of limited objective offensives; he kept strong combat and reconnaissance patrols forward of his lines constantly. But he always kept his perimeter intact, always maintained a reserve, and showed a marvellous ability for meeting strength with strength. The Japanese pattern of reinforcing Guadalcanal, and the impetuosity of Japanese leaders once they reached the island, played right into the American general's hands. Typically, a few thousand Japanese troops would be landed at night by Tanaka's Tokyo Express a few miles to either side of the Marine perimeter and they would attack almost without delay. The action would be furious at the point of contact, sometimes the Marine lines would be penetrated, but then the fire-brigade would arrive — a fresh infantry battalion, a platoon of tanks, the fire of an additional reinforcing artillery battalion, a flight of dive-bombers, perhaps all of these at once, and the Japanese would be thrown back, decimated by their own relentless courage in the face of killing fire.

The same fate that befell the Ichiki battalion was met by a 6,000-man brigade under Major-General Kiyotaki Kawaguchi, which landed on both sides of the 9,000-yard-wide perimeter in early September. The main body, about 4,000 men, mostly of the 124th Infantry, pressed inland under cover of the jungle to attack from the south against the inland perimeter toward the airfield.

That portion of the Marine line was thinly held, as the greatest danger was expected from attacks along the coast or from the sea.

Fortunately, Vandegrift had moved the original assault force at Tulagi across Sealark Channel to bolster the Marine defences. Combining the raider and parachute battalions under one commander, Colonel Merritt A. Edson, he placed this unit astride an open, grassy ridge that led directly to the division command post and the airfield. The 2nd Battalion, 5th Marines was one mile away in reserve and a battalion of 105-mm howitzers from the division's artillery regiment, the 11th Marines, was in direct support. The Kawaguchi Force lightly probed Edson's position on September 12, while a Japanese cruiser and several destroyers shelled Henderson Field, a frequent accompaniment to Japanese ground attacks. On the 13th, Edson tried a counterattack but was forced back to his original positions; the Japanese were too strong. That night, in a driving rain that severely limited visibility, the Japanese poured out of the jungle, smashing into the ridge position and forcing the American flanking companies back on the centre of the ridge. There the Marines held, the artillery smothered the attacking columns and troop assembly areas, and reinforcements from the 5th Marines joined the raiders and paratroopers in their foxholes. In the morning there was little left to do but mop up. Only about 500 of Kawaguchi's men struggled back alive through the jungle. A pair of diversionary attacks, mounted against the coastal perimeters while Kawaguchi struck, died in the face of stubborn Marine fire.

The Marines advance

On October 7, the Marines set out again in force with two battalions of the 5th Marines to engage the Japanese at the mouth of the Matanikau. Inland, two battalions of the 7th Marines, the 3rd Battalion, 2nd Marines, and the division's scout-sniper detachment were to drive west and then south after crossing the Matanikau upstream to pin the Japanese against the coast. Three battalions of artillery were in direct support of the attack. The advancing Marines ran into the Japanese 4th Infantry Regiment, which was also moving forward to the attack. The resulting action spread over two days in the rain-swept jungle. The Americans trapped one sizable pocket of Japanese near the coast; only a few escaped death. Another force of 1,500 men was isolated in a deep ravine inland.

There, while Marine riflemen on the high ground picked off the hapless enemy soldiers as they struggled up the steep slopes, artillery shells methodically blasted the floor of the ravine. Vandegrift broke off the action on October 9 when Intelligence indicated that a strong Japanese attack would be mounted from the Kokumbona area. When the Marine battalions retired to the perimeter, they took with them 65 dead and 125 wounded, but they left behind 700 Japanese dead.

The Intelligence was correct. General Hyakutake himself had landed on Guadalcanal on October 9 to take personal charge of the Japanese effort. He brought with him heavy reinforcements, the rest of the 2nd Division to join those elements already on the island, two battalions of the 38th Division, and more artillery. By mid-October, Hyakutake's strength was about

20,000 men, but Vandegrift had 23,000, for on October 13, the first American Army troops arrived on Guadalcanal, the 164th Infantry of the Americal Division from New Caledonia. The night after the 164th arrived, Japanese battleships fired a 90-minute bombardment against Henderson Field, partly to cover a daylight run of Tanaka's transports carrying Hyakutake's reinforcements. Although only 42 of Geiger's 90 planes were operational when the bombardment ended and Henderson Field was a shambles, the pilots used the fighter strip as soon as the sun rose and made the muddy runway firm enough to take off from.

Any plane that could carry a bomb or torpedo, including General Vandegrift's lumbering PBY flying boat, attacked the transports. Three were left burning and beached and the other two fled, but some 4,000 men of the 2nd Division were able to get ashore.

The battle for Bloody Ridge

On October 24, therefore, the 1st Battalion, 7th Marines held 2,500 yards of jungle front anchored on the ridge, now generally known as Edson's Ridge or Bloody Ridge, which the raiders and parachute troops had defended so gallantly in September. To the Marine battalion's left, the 2nd Battalion of the

164th Infantry held the portion of the line that curved back toward the coast. The two American battalions held the area that was to be the focal point of Japanese attacks. When Maruyama's soldiers surged forward from the jungle after nightfall on the 24th, they were met by a solid wall of Marine and Army small arms fire, canister shells from 37's, and a deadly rain of artillery and

mortar fire. As soon as it became apparent that the main thrust of the attack was aimed at Edson's Ridge, the 3rd Battalion, 164th Infantry, in reserve, was started forward to reinforce the Marines. Slipping and stumbling through the rainy darkness, the soldiers were fed into the Marine positions as they arrived and wherever they were needed. The lines held and they held again the next night as Maruyama made another attempt with his dwindling forces. Then it was over, and all Japanese attempts to penetrate the 1st Division's lines had failed; 3,500 of the enemy lay dead in, around, and in front of the American positions, including the 2nd Division's infantry group commander and two regimental commanders. One of these, Colonel Sejiro Furumiya of the 29th Infantry, had made a pledge to his men when they landed on Guadalcanal, that if they were unsuccessful in capturing the island "not even one man should expect to return alive".

Things were looking up for Vandegrift's troops. Despite the horrendous losses that the Allies had suffered in sea battles in the waters off Guadalcanal, a steady stream of supplies and men continued to be landed on the island under the protective cover of the "Cactus" pilots. And on October 18, the vibrant and aggressive Vice-Admiral William F. Halsey relieved Admiral Ghormley as Commander, South Pacific Area and brought with him a resolve that Guadalcanal would be held and the Japanese driven off. In that determination he was supported by President Roosevelt, who personally ordered the tempo of aid to the defenders to be stepped up. The 25th Infantry Division in Hawaii was alerted for a move to Guadalcanal, and the rest of the 2nd Marine Division and the Americal Division were also ordered

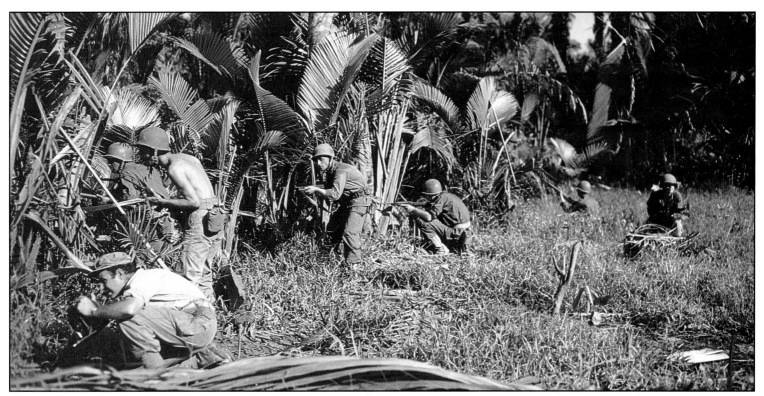

US forces advance during the Battle for Bloody Ridge.

forward.

Heartened by the promise of reinforcements, Vandegrift continued to keep the Japanese off balance with the troops he had. On November 3, six battalions under Colonel Edson probed forward and trapped a Japanese force near Point Cruz and eliminated another 300 men of Hyakutake's army. At the same time, on the eastern side of the perimeter, a reconnaissance in force by the 7th Marines, backed up by two battalions of the 164th Infantry, punished a 1,500-man Japanese reinforcement group from the 38th Division which landed near Koli Point, driving the enemy soldiers into the jungle. Partly as a result of this action, Hyakutake decided to abandon the concept of the

two-sided attack on the American position and ordered the 38th Division's troops to move overland to Kokumbona. Five hundred of the retreating Japanese failed to complete the trip. They were hunted down and killed by the Marines of the 2nd Raider Battalion who landed at Aola Bay 40 miles west of the Lunga on November 4. These men were part of a project dear to Admiral Turner's heart, an attempt to set up another airfield on Guadalcanal. Vandegrift wanted nothing to do with any scheme that dispersed American ground forces on Guadalcanal, but lost the argument to his naval superior. He did, however, get permission for the raiders to patrol overland to the Henderson Field perimeter and they accounted for the Japanese straggling through the jungle.

Reinforcements pour in

The further landing of 38th Division troops on Guadalcanal was part of a massive reinforcement effort which included the daylight landing of Japanese forces on November 14. While shore-based aircraft and planes from the carrier Enterprise sank seven of 11 transports carrying the Japanese soldiers, Tanaka's destroyers were able to rescue many of the men and Hyakutake had 10,000 fresh troops. But Vandegrift had two new reinforced regiments too, the 8th Marines from Samoa and the 182nd Infantry from New Caledonia, and he retained his numerical advantage. He continued to pressure the Japanese, repeatedly probing and jabbing toward Kokumbona in November, using many of his newly arrived Army and Marine battalions.

The Marine general needed the fresh men. His own division, after four months of fighting in the jungle heat and humidity, was worn out; over half the men had contracted malaria or other tropical diseases. His original Marine units had suffered nearly 2,000 casualties, 681 of them killed in action or dead of wounds. The decision was made to withdraw the 1st Marine Division to Australia for rest and rehabilitation. On December 9, 1942, General Vandegrift turned over command of the troops on Guadalcanal to Major-General Alexander M. Patch of the Americal Division, and the 5th Marines boarded ship to leave the island, leading the exodus of the 1st Division.

Patch's mission was to drive the Japanese off Guadalcanal, and his forces were increased substantially to give him the means to carry out this task. Major-General J. Lawton Collins' 25th Infantry Division began landing on Guadalcanal on December

17 and the last elements of the 2nd Marine Division came in on January 4 under command of Brigadier-General Alphonse de Carre. New Army and Marine squadrons swelled the ranks of the Cactus Air Force and the situation was grim indeed for the Japanese.

By the beginning of January, General Patch had 50,000 men of all services under his command. Hyakutake's 17th Army troops amounted to about 25,000 men, but they were now cut off from effective reinforcement or resupply by Allied air power and a resurgent naval effort. His men were on short rations and low on ammunition; many were sick with the same tropical diseases that had ravaged the Marines of Vandegrift's division, but there were not enough medical supplies to aid them back to health. While the Japanese were still capable of hard fighting, they could not sustain a serious offensive effort. The decision was made in Rabaul about mid-December to abandon the ill-fated attempt to recapture Guadalcanal and to rescue as many of Hyakutake's men as possible.

General Patch unwittingly reinforced the Japanese decision to get out. Commander since January 2 of a newly organised XIV Corps run by a skeletal staff from the Americal Division, he used his three divisions to drive unrelentingly west from the Lunga perimeter. Using Collins' 25th Division inland and de Carre's 2nd Division along the coast, he hammered steadily at the Japanese. The defenders fell back slowly, fighting hard but unable to hold any position long before the American troops, who used massive artillery, air, and naval gunfire support, drove them out. Kokumbona, so long the objective of Vandegrift's attacks, was occupied by the 25th Division on January 23. Here Patch held up the attack, anxious because reports of a Japanese shipping build-up at Rabaul and in the Shortland Islands presaged another attempt to take Guadalcanal. Actually, this was the Japanese destroyer force that was intended to evacuate Hyakutake's men.

Patch cautiously resumed his advance on January 30. He had a small blocking force in the mountain passes inland to prevent the Japanese crossing to the other side of the island, and he sent an Army battalion around Cape Esperance to the western coast to block that route of escape also. By February 5, when the advance was held up again by reports of a large Japanese flotilla lurking in the northern Solomons, the lead Army regiment, the 161st Infantry, had reached positions 3,500 yards west of Tassafaronga and only about 12 miles from Cape Esperance.

On the night of February 7–8, Japanese destroyers under the command of Rear-Admiral Koniji Koyonagi executed a masterly evacuation of 13,000 Japanese troops from Guadalcanal. Many of these men would fight the Americans again on other battlefields in the Solomons and on New Britain. But there were many others who would fight no more. Casualties had been high on both sides in this bitterly fought contest in the jungles and malaria infested swamps of Guadalcanal. However, thanks to their superior medical facilities and greater regard for human life, American casualties were correspondingly lower.

On January 8, 1943, the official ending of the Guadalcanal land campaign, General Patch could report "the complete and total defeat of Japanese forces on Guadalcanal." After the struggle for control of the island was decided, the Japanese never again

US marine displays his trophies and a Japanese marine flag.

advanced in the Pacific. The staggering Japanese losses of ships, planes, and pilots that were equally a feature of the Guadalcanal campaign with the bitter ground fighting were not replaceable in kind. Admiral Tanaka, whose Tokyo Express had done so much to sustain the Japanese on the island, considered that "Japan's doom was sealed with the closing of the struggle for Guadalcanal". The strategic initiative in the southwest Pacific now passed to the Allies, for good.

Allied public opinion did not attempt to conceal its disappointment, not to say impatience, at the results of Anglo-American strategy in the Mediterranean. As can well be imagined, political and military leaders in London and Washington were hardly able to pacify these frustrations by making public the vast organisation, training, and preparation then going on towards an operation which was to bear its first fruits at dawn on June 6. Certainly after five months of marking time the Allies scored a decisive victory over their enemy in Italy, but only less than 30 days before the Normandy landings and thus a little late in the day. The normal course of development of Allied strategy was hindered by a chain of unfortunate circumstances which, it must be said, had nothing to do with politics.

On January 16, 1944 the American 5th Army, still under the command of Lieutenant-General Mark Clark, renewed its attack on the Cassino redoubt, which was defended by XIV Panzer Corps from the 10th Army (General von Vietinghoff-Scheel). The main objective of this undertaking in such difficult terrain was to force Kesselring to move up the reinforcements at present around Rome to strengthen his front. When this had been achieved, the American VI Corps (Major-General John P. Lucas), which was to effect a surprise landing on the beaches at Anzio and Nettuno, would find the way open to drive inland and attack the enemy's communications. This was the fundamental idea of Operation "Shingle", a pet scheme of Churchill, who had succeeded in winning over both Roosevelt and Stalin. He had even agreed to sacrifice to it the amphibious forces collected together for a landing on Rhodes. Did Churchill see further than his Allies? It

seems likely that had the German 10th Army been annihilated during the first two weeks of February, nothing would have prevented Churchill from renewing his demands on his Allies and perhaps demanding an exploitation of this victory in the direction of Ljubljana and the abandonment of a landing in Provence, as planned at Teheran.

But everything was to go against him. First of all, General Clark considerably toned down the instructions given to him on January 12 by Sir Harold Alexander, commanding the 15th Army Group. Alexander saw the mission of the American VI Corps as follows: "to cut the enemy's main communications in the Colli Laziali (Alban Hills) area south-east of Rome, and threaten the rear of the XIV German Corps". Clark's directive of the same date to General Lucas merely required him "to seize and secure a beachhead in the vicinity of Anzio" and thence "to advance on the Colli Laziali".

This threefold manoeuvre (seize, secure, and advance) clearly did not reflect Alexander's original intention, but Alexander did not order Clark to change his directive so as to bring it into line with his own. As we shall see him giving in to his subordinate again on the following May 26, we can take it that it was not merely an oversight. We must believe that in acting as he did, General Clark was still under the strain of the Salerno landings, though he says nothing of this in his memoirs. John Lucas, entrusted with carrying out Operation "Shingle", noted in his diary: "It will be worse than the Dardanelles". His friend George S. Patton, spitting fire and smelling a fight in the offing, had said to him:

Allied landing ship unloads supplies.

"'John, there is no one in the Army I would hate to see killed as much as you, but you can't get out of this alive. Of course, you might be badly wounded. No one ever blames a wounded general!' He advised Lucas to read the Bible when the going got tough, and then turned to one of the VI Corps commander's aides and said, 'Look here; if things get too bad, shoot the old man in the backside; but don't you dare kill the man!'"

About a week before D-day, an ill-fated landing exercise hastily carried out in the Gulf of Salerno only served to confirm Major-General Lucas's pessimistic forecast.

The Anzio landings

No other landing in Europe or the Pacific was initially as successful, and at such little cost, as that at Anzio-Nettuno in Operation "Shingle". By midnight on January 22, that is after 22 hours of operations, Rear-Admirals Frank J. Lowry of the U.S. Navy and Thomas H. Troubridge of the Royal Navy had landed 36,034 men, 3,069 vehicles, and 90 per cent of the assault equipment of the U.S. VI Corps. This comprised the British 1st Division (Major-General W. Penney), the American 3rd Division (Major-General L. K. Truscott), a regiment and a battalion of paratroops, three battalions of Rangers, and a brigade of Commandos. Losses amounted to 13 killed, 44 missing, and 97 wounded. The supporting naval forces, four light cruisers and 24 destroyers, had neutralised the fire of the shore batteries and two German battalions had been overrun on the beaches. "And that was all," wrote General Westphal as he reckoned up his weak forces. "There was nothing else in the area we could have thrown

against the enemy on that same day. The road to Rome (37 miles) was now open. No-one could have prevented a force which drove on hard from entering the Eternal City. For two days after the landing we were in a breath-taking situation. Our counter-measures could only take effect after 48 hours."

Kesselring musters his strength

The General Staff of Army Group "C" had made several studies of a possible Allied landing of some strategic importance. For each hypothesis envisaged (Istria, Ravenna, Civitavecchia, Leghorn, Viareggio), the formations which would fight it had been detailed off, the routes they would have to take marked out, and their tasks laid down. Each hypothetical situation had been given a keyword. Kesselring only had to signal "Fall Richard" for the following to converge on the Anzio bridgehead:

1. the "Hermann Göring" Panzer Division from the area of Frosinone and the 4th Parachute Division from Terni, both in I Parachute Corps (General Schlemm)

2. from the Sangro front LXXVI Panzer Corps (General Herr: 26th Panzer and 3rd Panzergrenadier Divisions); from the Garigliano front the 29th Panzergrenadier Division, newly arrived in the sector; and

3. from northern Italy the staff of the 14th Army and the 65th and 362nd Divisions which had crossed the Apennines as quickly as the frost and snow would allow them.

But O.K.W. intervened and ordered Field-Marshal von Rundstedt to hand over to Kesselring the 715th Division, then stationed in the Marseilles area, and Colonel-General Löhr,

Allied landing ship loaded with supplies. Anzio Harbour, Italy.

commanding in the Balkans, to send him his 114th Jäger Division.

On January 23, when Colonel-General von Mackensen arrived to take charge of operations against the Allied forces, all that lay between Anzio and Rome was a detachment of the "Hermann Göring" Panzer Division and a hotchpotch of artillery ranging from the odd 8.8-cm A.A. to Italian, French, and Yugoslav field guns. Despite the talents of Kesselring as an improviser and the capabilities of his general staff, a week was to pass before the German 14th Army could offer any consistent opposition to the Allied offensive.

On the Allied side, however, Major-General John P. Lucas

thought only of consolidating his bridgehead and getting ashore the balance of his corps, the 45th Division (Major-General W. Eagles) and the 1st Armoured Division (Major-General E. N. Harmon). It will be recognised that in so doing he was only carrying out the task allotted to the 5th Army. On January 28. his 1st Armoured Division had indeed captured Aprilia, over ten miles north of Anzio, but on his right the American 3rd Division had been driven back opposite Cisterna. On the same day Mackensen had three divisions in the line and enough units to make up a fourth; by the last day of the month he was to have eight.

Was a great strategic opportunity lost between dawn on January 22 and twilight on the 28th? In London Churchill was

German self propelled gun and tank.

champing with impatience and wrote to Sir Harold Alexander: "I expected to see a wild cat roaring into the mountains and what do I find? A whale wallowing on the beaches!"

Returning to the subject in his memoirs, Churchill wrote: "The spectacle of 18,000 vehicles accumulated ashore by the fourteenth day for only 70,000 men, or less than four men to a vehicle, including drivers and attendants … was astonishing."

Churchill might perhaps be accused of yielding too easily to the spite he felt at the setbacks of Operation "Shingle", for which he had pleaded so eagerly to Stalin and Roosevelt. These were, however, not the feelings of the official historian of the U.S. Navy who wrote ten years after the event:

"It was the only amphibious operation in that theater where the Army was unable promptly to exploit a successful landing, or where the enemy contained Allied forces on a beachhead for a prolonged period. Indeed, in the entire war there is none to compare with it; even the Okinawa campaign in the Pacific was shorter."

We would go along with this statement, implying as it does that the blame lay here, were it not for General Truscott's opinion, which is entirely opposed to Morison's quoted above. Truscott lived through every detail of the Anzio landings as commander of the 3rd Division, then as second-in-command to General Lucas, whom he eventually replaced. He was recognised by his fellow-officers as a first-class leader, resolute, aggressive, and very competent. His evidence is therefore to be reckoned with:

"I suppose that armchair strategists will always labour under the delusion that there was a 'fleeting opportunity' at Anzio during which some Napoleonic figure would have charged over the Colli Laziali (Alban Hills), played havoc with the German line of communications, and galloped on into Rome. Any such concept betrays lack of comprehension of the military problem involved. It was necessary to occupy the Corps Beachhead Line to prevent the enemy from interfering with the beaches, otherwise enemy artillery and armoured detachments operating against the flanks could have cut us off from the beach and prevented the unloading of troops, supplies, and equipment. As it was, the Corps Beachhead Line was barely distant enough to prevent direct artillery fire on the beaches.

"On January 24th (i.e. on D+2) my division, with three Ranger battalions and the 504th Parachute Regiment attached, was extended on the Corps Beachhead Line, over a front of twenty miles … Two brigade groups of the British 1st Division held a front of more than seven miles."

In his opinion again the Allied high command overestimated the psychological effect on the enemy's morale of the simple news of an Anglo-American landing behind the 10th Army. This is shown by the text of a leaflet dropped to German troops, pointing out the apparently impossible strategic situation in which they were now caught, pinned down at Cassino and outflanked at Anzio, and urging them to surrender.

Kesselring beats Alexander to the punch

But far from allowing himself to be intimidated, Kesselring assembled his forces with a promptness underestimated by Alexander and Clark. Another reason why he was able to race them to it was because the latter were somewhat short of matériel for amphibious operations. The figures speak for themselves: on June 6, 1944 for a first wave of 12 divisions Eisenhower had 3,065 landing craft, whereas Anzio had 237 for four divisions.

Under these conditions, even if Lucas had had the temperament of a Patton, one could hardly have expected him to throw his forces into an attack on the Colli Laziali, over 20 miles from Anzio, with the two divisions of his first echelon and not worry also about his flanks and communications. Finally, Lucas did not have this cavalier temperament, and the day after the landings he noted in his diary: "The tension in a battle like this is terrible. Who the hell would be a general?"

Enter Hitler

The chances lost here, however, were to give rise during the months of February and March to two of the most furious battles of the war. They both ended in defeat for the attacker. On February 29 Mackensen had to abandon his attempt to crush the Anzio beach-head and Clark reported that his repeated attempts to force the Cassino defile had failed.

The battle for the beach-head arose from Hitler's initiative. On January 28 he sent Kesselring the following directive, which is worth quoting in full, so well does it reveal the Führer's state of mind on the day after the disasters suffered by Army Group

"South" on the Dniepr at Kanev, and at a time when everyone was expecting an Anglo-American attack across the Channel.

"In a few days from now," he wrote, "the 'Battle for Rome' will start: this will decide the defence of Central Italy and the fate of the 10th Army. But it has an even greater significance, for the Nettuno landing is the first step of the invasion of Europe planned for 1944.

"The enemy's aim is to pin down and to wear out major German forces as far as possible from the English base in which the main body of the invasion force is being held in a constant state of readiness, and to gain experience for their future operations.

"The significance of the battle to be fought by the 14th Army must be made clear to each one of its soldiers.

"It will not be enough to give clear and correct tactical orders. The army, the air force, and the navy must be imbued with a fanatical determination to come out victorious from this battle and to hang on until the last enemy soldier has been exterminated or driven back into the sea. The men will fight with a solemn hatred against an enemy who is waging a relentless war of extermination against the German people, an enemy to whom everything seems a legitimate means to this end, an enemy who, in the absence of any high ethical intention, is plotting the destruction of Germany and, along with her, that of European civilisation. The battle must be hard and without pity, and not only against the enemy but also against any leader of men who, in this decisive hour, shows any sign of weakness.

"As in Sicily, on the Rapido, and at Ortona, the enemy must

be shown that the fighting strength of the German Army is still intact and that the great invasion of 1944 will be an invasion which will drown in the blood of the Anglo-Saxon soldiers."

That is why the German 14th Army, whilst it drove off the repeated attempts of the U.S. VI Corps to break out from Aprilia and to cut off the Rome-Gaeta railway at Campoleone, actively prepared to go over to the counter-attack as ordered. On February 10 a counterattack led by the 3rd Panzergrenadier Division (Lieutenant-General Grdser) retook the station at Carroceto. That day the German communiqué announced 4,000 prisoners taken since January 22, whereas the Allies' figure was only 2,800. Rightly alarmed by these setbacks, General Clark sent the British 56th Division (Major-General Templer) into the bridgehead; also, at Alexander's suggestion, he appointed Truscott second-in-command of VI Corps. Meanwhile Colonel-General von Mackensen had been called to O.K.W. to put his plan for a counter-offensive before the Führer. The latter offered no objection when Mackensen explained his idea of driving his attack along the Albano–Anzio line, with diversionary attacks on either side. Hitler did not stop there, however, but took it upon himself to interfere in every detail of the plan, from which he expected wonders. Mackensen thus saw the front on which he was to attack, the troops he was to use, and even the deployment these forces were to adopt, all altered by Hitler.

The operation was entrusted to LXXVI Panzer Corps. It was to attack on a front of less than four miles with two divisions up and the 26th Panzergrenadier Division (Lieutenant-General von Lüttwitz) and the 20th Panzergrenadier Division (Lieutenant-

General Fries) in army reserve. Hitler ordered this so the infantry could be given supporting fire that would pulverise the enemy's defences. Mackensen tried in vain to point out that such a massive concentration would present a sitting target to the Anglo-American air forces and that Luftflotte II, under the command of Field-Marshal von Richthofen, did not have the means to fight them off. It was no good. Hitler also refused to listen to the argument that it was useless lining up the guns wheel to wheel with insufficient ammunition for them to fire at the required rate.

The attack started on February 16 as ordered by Hitler. There was a preliminary softening up by 300 guns, but the 114th and 715th Divisions, which were to advance side by side, were to be denied the support of a creeping barrage. The spongy ground of the Pontine marshes prevented the tanks and the assault guns, which were to support the waves of infantry, from getting off the roads. The 14th Army's offensive might have had the intermittent support of 20 to 30 Luftwaffe fighter-bombers, but the German troops on the ground had to withstand the assault of no less than 1,100 tons of bombs. The Anglo-American tactical air forces boxed in the battlefield and considerably hindered the movement of supplies up towards the 14th Army's front line units.

By nightfall LXXVI Panzer Corps had advanced some three to four miles into the Allied lines and was about seven to eight miles from its objective of Anzio-Nettuno. Its guns had fired 6,500 shells, but had received ten times as many. For three days Mackensen attempted to regain the upper hand, but in vain: Truscott, who had just relieved Lucas, was too vigilant for him. On February 29, 1 Parachute Corps took up the attack again in

US troops in a foxhole Anzio-Nettuno beachhead.

the Cisterna area, but this came to a halt a few hundred yards from its point of departure. The battle around the bridgehead died down and General Clark reinforced the position with the British 5th and the American 34th Divisions. The beaches and the Allies' rear positions continued to be harassed by German heavy artillery with its observation posts up in the Colli Laziali. A huge 11-inch railway gun in particular played havoc among the defenders. The air force was unable to silence it since, as soon as it had fired, "Leopold", as its crew, or "Anzio Annie", as the Allies called it, withdrew into a tunnel near Castel Gandolfo.

At sea, Operation "Shingle" cost Admiral Sir John Cunningham, C.-in-C. Mediterranean, the light cruisers Spartan and Penelope and three destroyers, all of the Royal Navy. Amongst the weapons used by the Germans were glide bombs and human torpedoes, the latter making their first appearance with the Kriegsmarine.

Tank positions itself to attack Japanese positions on 'Hill 1070'.

By May 1942, the Japanese had reached the limits they had set themselves in South-East Asia. They had driven the British from Burma and now prepared to go over to the defensive. The British forces under General Wavell, the Commander-in-Chief in India, took this opportunity to attack, and a series of campaigns began which eventually brought about the final Japanese surrender. The fighting in Burma often seemed isolated from the rest of the war, for it had its own momentum, set by the monsoon rains and enormous supply problems.

It was on September 17, 1942, that Wavell despatched from India an operation instruction to the G.O.C.-in-C. Eastern Army, Lieutenant-General N. M. S. Irwin, which gave the objects for the army in the 1942–1943 dry season (October–May): first to develop communications for the purpose of reconquering Burma and opening the Burma Road; and second to bring the Japanese to battle in order to use up their strength, especially in the air.

Wavell gave four objectives as his immediate intention in order to attain these ends:

1. to capture Akyab and reoccupy the upper Arakan;

2. to strengthen British positions in the Chin hills;

3. to occupy Kalewa and Sittaung on the Chindwin; and thence to raid Japanese lines of communication (Wavell had already given Brigadier Orde Wingate orders to raise and train a Long Range Penetration Brigade for this purpose); and

4. to make necessary administrative arrangements to allow for a rapid advance into upper or lower Burma should opportunity offer.

We are here immediately concerned with the first objective, the British attempt to capture Akyab in the dry season 1942–43. Throughout this narrative it is important to remember that the Japanese forces in the Arakan were seasoned victorious soldiers, whereas their British and Indian opponents were raw, inexperienced troops, often new recruits.

The Japanese 213th Regiment in the Arakan, under the command of Colonel K. Miyawaki and consisting of two battalions (II/213th and III/213th), had moved into Akyab during the summer of 1942 after chasing the British/Indian forces from Yenangyaung, Myingan, Monywa, Shwegyin, and finally Kalewa, which it had captured on May 11. The 33rd Division, of which it formed a part, had advanced from Siam for the initial invasion of Burma, but the 213th Regiment had been left in Siam and had not rejoined its division until after the fall of Rangoon. It was, therefore, the freshest regiment and had had the fewest casualties in the conquest of Burma and was full of fight.

As the British/Indian 14th Division started its southward advance from Chittagong to Cox's Bazar and beyond, Miyawaki in mid-October sent his II/213th battalion up the Mayu river by launch to occupy the line Buthidaung — "Tunnels" Road — Maungdaw, where first contact was made with the 1/15th Punjab battalion on October 23. The "Tunnels" Road was the only all-weather road in the area in 1942.

On September 21 Lieutenant-General Irwin had ordered the 14th Indian Division, commanded by Major-General W. L. Lloyd, to move towards Akyab to forestall the Japanese arrival on the Buthidaung–Maungdaw line.

Earlier in the year the 14th Division had been earmarked for operations in Burma, but the fall of Rangoon had prevented its arrival. After the British defeat in Burma a special committee had reported that one of the reasons for this defeat was the overmodernisation of Indian divisions. Certain divisions were, therefore, reorganised to become "light divisions" with their transport mainly on a jeep and animal basis. The 14th Division, which had recently been responsible for the defence of Bengal, Bihar, and Orissa, was not so reorganised.

This division consisted of four brigades (47th, 55th, 88th, and 123rd), with two British and ten Indian battalions plus one British field regiment and one Indian mountain regiment of artillery. The Indian battalions came mainly from the dry areas of the Punjab, Baluchistan, and Rajputana and were unused to the hot, steamy, malarial swamps of the Arakan. Later another brigade joined the division. For this rôle the 14th Division was supported by a special reconnaissance force ("V" Force) hidden, with its wireless sets, in the hills, and No. 2000 Flotilla, a scratch collection of steamboats, launches, and sampans, to help the units across and down the rivers and to supply them.

The Arakan, on Burma's north-west coast, is a country of steep, densely-forested hill ranges up to 2,000 feet high, running parallel from north to south, separated by narrow cultivated valleys filled with rice fields, mangroves, and tidal creeks. The coastal strip from Maungdaw to the tip of the Mayu peninsula, Foul Point, opposite Akyab Island, is 45 miles long and ten miles wide in the north but tapers down to a few hundred yards wide at Foul Point.

To the east winds the Mayu river (called the Kalapanzin in its upper reaches), flanked by swamps of elephant grass and bamboo, and divided by knife-edged limestone ridges, 150 feet high.

East of the Mayu valley rises the great jumbled mass of the Arakan Tracts, reaching as far as the Kaladan river valley, and 2,500 feet high. Further east again are the Arakan Yomas.

In the dry season, fair-weather tracks for wheeled vehicles can be made over the dry paddy fields and along the coastal strip at low tide. From mid-May to October the annual 200-inch rainfall is almost unceasing, with malaria and other tropical diseases hyperendemic. In the dry season from November to March the weather is delightful.

As it advanced, the 14th Division's line of communication from railhead was by sea from Chittagong to Cox's Bazar, motor transport to Tumbru, sampans on the Naf river to Bawli Bazar, and pack transport onwards.

In spite of reinforcements of motor launches, landing craft, and three paddle-steamers given to him, Major-General Lloyd by November 17 could still guarantee the maintenance of only four battalions to attack the Japanese. Being able to apply superior strength was always a problem for the British in the Arakan.

The Japanese, although outnumbered, were much better trained in watermanship and were thus able to take full advantage of all types of river transport, especially as Akyab Island was at the hub of the river system running north. Thus their water communication could easily be switched from one valley to another, whereas the British lines of approach were divided by virtually inaccessible ridges.

In December 1942, the Japanese air situation in the south-west

Three mobile guns take up positions.

Pacific had become so grave that two Japanese air brigades were despatched from Burma, leaving the 5th Air Division with only about 50 fighters and 90 medium bombers available for the whole of the Burma front-to meet a growing Allied air strength.

No. 224 Group, R.A.F., consisting of six Hawker Hurricane squadrons, two light bomber squadrons of Bristol Blenheims and Bisleys, and one Beaufighter squadron (totalling about 120 aircraft), was ordered to support the 14th Division's advance. But at that time these squadrons had not been trained in close air support, the Hurricanes were not fitted with bomb racks, and there were no ground controllers with the brigades, so the group's efforts were initially of little value to the infantry (especially in comparison with later operations). Thus the group's aircraft were used chiefly for interdiction along the sparse Japanese supply routes, including the sea-lanes to Akyab. In fact, during the first year the R.A.F. had very little effect on the ground campaign apart from moral support by the sound of the engines. Except at high altitude the Hurricane was no match for the Mitsubishi A6M Zero, and the R.A.F. had no long-range fighters available to sustain an offensive against the Japanese air bases. In spite of this the R.A.F. did slowly begin to win air superiority, which made efficient close air support, as well as vital air supply, possible later.

All these administrative and training shortcomings of the British forces must be remembered, as otherwise it is difficult to understand how Colonel Miyawaki, with a maximum of only

Bren Carrier crosses ditch at full speed and charges into action, Arakan.

two battalions on the mainland, could hold up 12 battalions of infantry supported by six batteries of artillery for a period of 13 weeks from first contact on October 23 to January 22 1943, when the first detachments of the 55th Division started to arrive in the Akyab area. The difficulty Lloyd had was to apply his strength.

Irwin's original plan was for a seaborne landing on Akyab accompanied by a land advance down the Mayu peninsula to Foul Point. But by the end of October Wavell came to the conclusion that a direct seaborne attack in which transport and warships would be exposed to heavy air attack for a minimum of three days was no longer practicable.

Irwin therefore decided to use the 6th Infantry Brigade Group

from the British 2nd Division to land on Akyab Island with the help of five motor launches, 72 landing craft, and three paddle-steamers which Admiral Sir James Somerville had placed at his disposal, as soon as Lloyd had advanced to Foul Point. The speed of the overland advance was therefore vital.

However, Irwin postponed Lloyd's advance to the attack in order to give him time to improve his communications, so that he could bring an extra brigade to bear. This delayed Lloyd by three weeks so that just when he was about to attack, Miyawaki withdrew his II/213th battalion facing Lloyd to a general line Gwedauk–Kondon, thus drawing Lloyd further away from his base.

Lloyd finally made contact again on December 22, when he

attacked on either side of the Mayu range and also detached one battalion to the Kaladan river. The Japanese repulsed all attacks but the wide front forced Miyawaki to commit his only other battalion, the III/213th, on December 29. Further British attacks were repulsed. The confident Japanese, having now got a measure of their enemy, started to harass Lloyd's two forward brigades by small patrol attacks at night and sudden bombardments from mortars, which startled these inexperienced troops and led them to believe that there were many more Japanese opposing them than just two battalions. Miyawaki, however, during this period took the risk of leaving the defence of Akyab Island to his antiaircraft gunners, supported by administrative personnel.

During a visit with Wavell to the Donbaik front on December 10, Irwin criticised Lloyd for dispersing his force so widely that he had insufficient strength on the coast. He ordered Lloyd to concentrate and break through at Donbaik.

However, two more attacks by the 14th Division on their two objectives, Rathedaung and Donbaik, during the first two weeks in January, again failed. Repeated attacks by fresh troops on January 18 and 19 also failed with comparatively heavy losses.

But early in January, Lieutenant-General Shojiro Iida, commanding the 15th Army, realising the importance of, and threat to, Akyab ordered Lieutenant-General Takishi Koga to move his 55th Division to hold Akyab. The 55th Division was a battle-trained formation which had fought in China and then advanced from Siam to Burma in 1942. During the previous year, it had fought through from Moulmein in the south via Pegu, Toungoo, and Mandalay to Bhamo and the Chinese frontier.

Koga ordered a rapid overland advance via Pakokku to the Kaladan valley on the one hand, whilst at the same time opening up an administrative sea route from Toungup to Akyab. He ordered Miyawaki's 213th Regiment to hold the Rathedaung–Laungchaung–Donbaik line at all costs. On January 22 No. 224 Group R.A.F. attacked the Japanese columns on the Pakokku trail.

Irwin reinforced Lloyd with two fresh brigades, artillery, and eight Valentine tanks. On February 1, after a heavy but badly co-ordinated R.A.F. bombardment, these fresh troops with the Valentines attacked the Japanese dug-in position at Donbaik, but after repeated assaults and heavy casualties over two days, were thrown back. Two days later similar frontal attacks on Rathedaung also failed.

The Japanese had won the race to Akyab, for by the end of February Koga had assembled the whole of the 55th Division, less one battalion, in that area.

Iida expected Koga to consolidate, but the latter saw the six British/Indian brigades under Lloyd split up by rivers and ranges into three quite separate identities, with his own forces holding a central position at the confluence of the Arakan rivers. Koga saw an excellent opportunity to counter-attack these tired brigades and destroy them piecemeal.

Koga laid a three-phase plan. First, the enemy forces in the Kaladan valley were to be overwhelmed by the "Miyawaki" Column (one infantry battalion and one mountain artillery battalion). Then the brigade east of the Mayu river was to be encircled by the "Tanahashi" Column (two infantry battalions and one mountain regiment) operating from Rathedaung and supported by a flank advance by Miyawaki from the Kaladan. Finally, the combined forces of this right hook, resupplied by launches moving up the Mayu, would cross the river and the Mayu range to seize Indin. This would cut off the British/Indian brigades threatening the Donbaik–Laungchaung line. Koga left one battalion to hold Akyab and three battalions ("Uno" Column) to hold the Mayu peninsula.

Meanwhile, Lloyd was reorganising for another attack on Donbaik, but Irwin, aware of supply difficulties and danger from the east flank, ordered him to withdraw, intending to replace his division with the 26th. However, Wavell, egged on by Churchill, felt that it was essential for the morale of the whole Indian Army to score some sort of victory, rather than ignominiously retreat after suffering, by European standards, quite minor casualties. On February 26 Wavell directed Irwin to order Lloyd to attack Donbaik again with two brigades and to destroy "the numerically insignificant opposition". Irwin delayed the attack but also the withdrawal. At this time Irwin sent Slim, then commanding XV Corps in India, to visit the front and report on the situation. He later told Irwin that Lloyd's command was now far too large for a single divisional headquarters, and that Lloyd's tactics were too obviously frontal (a reflection on Irwin's own instructions). But Irwin did not place Slim in command of operations, nor heed his advice.

By February 21 the first phase of Koga's plan started. By March 7 the "Miyawaki" Column had cleared the Kaladan valley as far as Kyauktaw, and "Tanahashi" Column had captured Rathedaung. The British/Indian 6th Brigade, with six battalions, obeyed

Wavell's orders and carried out, a deliberate attack on March 18 on the "Uno" Column dug in at Donbaik, but fell back after receiving only 300 casualties out of the 6,000-strong attacking force. With the "Miyawaki" and "Tanahashi" Columns now poised on the east bank of the Mayu river, and the "Uno" Column as the anvil, having withstood the British attack at Donbaik, Koga launched the third phase of his attack, starting on the night March 24–25. He called for and was given all available air support from the 5th Air Division.

Tanahashi sent one battalion north-west, which cut the coastal road at Gyindaw, whilst he, with the remaining two battalions of his force, advanced on Indin. In spite of a strenuous counter-attack and exhortations from their commanders, the brigades of the 14th Division on the coastal plain were unable to stop Tanahashi, who occupied Indin on April 6, thus cutting off 11 British/Indian battalions and attached troops south of that point. After an attack by a third brigade from the north had failed to remove this block, the 6th Brigade managed to escape with its transport along the beach at low tide. but the 47th Brigade had to leave all its transport and guns and retreat in small dispersal groups through the jungle. Lieutenant-General Koga had completed his three-phase encirclement of the British/Indian brigades in one calendar month, exactly according to plan, and had inflicted severe casualties on a much larger force. With seven battalions and one pack regiment of artillery he had temporarily destroyed the 47th Brigade and defeated the 4th, 6th, and 71st Brigades with their three regiments of artillery (totalling seven British and ten Indian battalions).

Landing craft unloading at Letpan.

With the arrival of his fresh II/214th battalion, which completed the strength of his division, Koga, who saw his enemy reeling, asked Iida if he could continue to attack until the monsoon. Iida, who trusted Koga, gave him carte blanche.

Meanwhile, Lloyd had been replaced by Major-General C. E. N. Lomax and his 26th Division headquarters. Lieutenant-General Slim, commander of XV Indian Corps, whose duties during the past seven months had been to suppress the vicious insurgency campaign in Bengal led by the Indian Congress Party, which had stated categorically that they would prefer Japanese to British rule, was placed in overall command of the Arakan front on April 5. Slim had been in active command of the British/Indian forces in their 1,000-mile retreat from Burma the previous year and, as was his wont, had learnt much from his victorious, pugnacious enemy, who was trained to expect to fight against all odds. Slim found a most unsatisfactory state of affairs. Most of the units now under command of the 26th Division had had their morale lowered by abortive attacks on Rathedaung and Donbaik, and then had been eased out of their own defensive positions by the Japanese capacity for manoeuvres, flank attacks, and ability to bring all their weapons and troops, however inferior in numbers, to bear at a decisive point. All units, especially the Indian ones, were frustrated and bewildered and, as the British official history states, "the morale of the troops was generally poor and in some units very low".

Slim ordered Lomax to hold the Maungdaw–"Tunnels"–Buthidaung line. He reinforced Lomax's four brigades (4th, 6th, 55th, and 71st) with the 36th Brigade, bringing the force to a total of 19 battalions including seven British, 11 Indian, and one Gurkha.

Meanwhile, General Koga had eight battalions available for attack. He left one battalion to contain the British forces on the coastal strip, and one battalion with a mountain artillery regiment ("Miyawaki" Column) to hold his enemy east of the Mayu river. He divided his remaining six battalions, each supported by pack artillery, into "Uno" and "Tanahashi" Columns, and gave them the task of seizing Buthidaung and the Tunnels line and then wheeling left to capture Maungdaw. At this juncture the "Miyawaki" Column, east of the Mayu, would advance due north and capture Taung Bazar. The Japanese started their advance on April 23.

The "Uno" Column met with stubborn resistance at Kanthe, so the "Tanahashi" Column by-passed Kanthe by advancing along the razor beak Mayu range and seized Point 551 overlooking the Tunnels area of the Maungdaw–Buthidaung Road. Lomax cleverly formed an open box to trap the advancing Japanese between his 4th and 6th Brigades to the west, 55th Brigade to the east, and 71st Brigade to the north, forming the lid. The Japanese, however, launched their northward drive in earnest on May 2 and, by May 3, the sides of the box had crumbled and the lid had opened "without adequate reason". The plan was a good one, but the training and morale of the British/Indian troops inevitably led to its failure.

As Buthidaung and the Tunnels area fell to the Japanese, Slim, realising how badly his superior forces had once again been defeated in the jungle, wanted to retreat 60 miles back to Cox's

7th Division fights its way out of Japanese encirclement.

Bazar, with the intention of luring the Japanese forces into open country where his troops could oppose them on ground more suitable to their training and armament, and at the same time stretch and expose the enemy's communications.

Irwin, however, opposed this plan and ordered Slim to hold the line Bawli Bazar–Goppe Bazar–Taung Bazar, only 20 miles north of the line Maungdaw–Buthidaung, and gave Lomax a sixth brigade, with orders to prepare a counter-attack to retake Maungdaw by surprise.

British operations in the Arakan ended in May 1943 with their forces back on their start-line and the stubborn and mistaken Irwin, who had wished to sack Slim, being sacked himself.

By May 11 General Koga had again won a striking victory over superior forces. The partial failure of the British demolition plan, and the disappearance in panic of all the civilian labour on which the British/Indian forces relied overmuch, resulted in very large quantities of booty falling into his hands. In view of the depth of the British retreat and the arrival of the monsoon, Koga decided to take up a defensive position on the general line Buthidaung–Maungdaw with five battalions and a regiment of artillery and withdraw the remainder of his division to Akyab for rest and recuperation. In 16 weeks he had caused his enemy to suffer over 5,000 battle casualties.

The news of the British failure in the Arakan, resulting in the loss of Buthidaung and Maungdaw, reached Washington just when the "Trident" Conference, which had been called to decide on future Allied policy in South-East Asia, was taking place. General Wavell, the Indian Army commander, and the commanders in the Arakan all came under most severe criticism. Churchill ordered that new commanders must be found and battalions whose morale had broken should be severely disciplined. If, he said, Indian Army troops were incapable of fighting in the jungle, commando formations should be formed as a prototype and an example to show them how to fight. Answers from India were that the Indian Army had been grossly over-expanded since Pearl Harbor and the best Indian units were in the Middle East, leaving a "second class army" to oppose the Japanese. Jungle fighting required, above all, good infantry but the infantry had also been milked of its best and most intelligent men to form technical corps like the expanded Indian artillery, previously manned wholly by the British. Indian troops had had their loyalty undermined by subversion from the newly formed Indian Independence League with its Indian National Army fighting alongside the Japanese. British officers drafted into the Indian Army had not had time to learn the language and get to know their men. Reinforcements to replace battle and malarial casualties had arrived piecemeal and many of them half- trained. Some units had been left in the front line for many months without relief. Congress-sponsored riots in August and September 1942, accompanied by maldistribution of food as a result of their depredations and destruction of communications, resulted in widespread famine in which 4 million had died, and this led to a disaffection amongst reinforcements moving through these areas to the battle line, so that they spread subversion amongst the forward troops.

Wavell was only too well aware that the failure in the Arakan, following as it did the disastrous campaigns in Malaya and Burma, had dealt the army in India a severe shock. Yet he knew that the Japanese were not "invincible" and had shown grave weaknesses of which advantage could be taken by a better trained army reinforced with self-confidence and self-respect. One undoubted advantage gained by the British was that during the year the R.A.F. had begun to attain air superiority throughout the whole front. This in itself could be made into a battle-winning factor. The success of the first Chindit operation, with its total reliance on air supply, offset the failures in the Arakan and pointed the way to victory in the future.

Wavell appointed a special committee to report on the readiness for war of British and Indian infantry battalions in India, and to make recommendations for improvement.

A new command set-up was created. Wavell was promoted Viceroy of India to look after the civil side and to see that the population would support its armed forces. General Sir Claude Auchinleck was recalled from the Middle East to be C.-in-C. India and to make the Indian sub-continent into an efficient administrative and training base from which the fighting forces could draw their strength. He eventually created a self-confident new model Indian Army which had become one of the best fighting machines in the world by 1945.

Lord Louis Mountbatten, who had previously been head of Combined Operations in Britain, was now appointed Allied

Supreme Commander, South-East Asia Command, with his headquarters in Ceylon. Under him was a new 11th Army Group (General Sir George Giffard), and under Giffard a new 14th Army (Lieutenant-General Slim) responsible for operations in Burma. Additionally XV Corps, under Lieutenant-General A. F. P. Christison, operating in the Arakan, came under Slim's command.

Brigades were to be formed of one British, one Indian, and one Gurkha battalion. Much more reliance was to be placed on the redoubtable Gurkhas, who had been represented by only one battalion in the Arakan débâcle.

After the first Chindit operation had proved the reliability of air supply, this form of support would be developed and taught to all units so that they need never retreat or disintegrate if the Japanese got behind them.

The R.A.F. was persuaded to co-operate more fully in developing more reliable and accurate close air support for the army involving more intimate mutual signal arrangements and co-operation so that aircraft could take the place of artillery where necessary in the deep jungle.

All ranks were given more jungle, river, and night training in order that these seemingly hostile circumstances could be used to the men's positive advantage rather than handicapping them as in the past.

Rations and methods of cooking in the forward areas were improved so that detachments could fend for themselves for many weeks, and special rations were issued during training to build up men before operations so that they were capable of enduring long periods of duress.

Malaria, which was causing a hundred times more casualties than bullets or shells, was tackled by mepacrine, strict anti-malarial measures, and forward malarial treatment centres so that men needing treatment were not evacuated to base areas but remained in the line as a reserve to protect communications. This reform was one of the most effective means of ensuring that battalions in the line maintained their strength.

An illustration of the disproportionate losses from diseases is the British XXXIII Corps' casualty figures for June to November 1944, which were typical of all formations in this theatre:

Battle casualties   3,289

Sickness   47,098 (including 20,430 malaria cases).

These remedial actions have been emphasised because they were to turn the scales in the Arakan in 1944 when the Japanese for a third time launched their short range penetration forces with again, it must be added, numerically very much inferior forces. Also it must be remembered that if the Japanese had had air superiority and as good air support, air supply, and intercommunication as the British were to enjoy, the outcome might have been very different.

Preparations for Chindit expedition, mule is loaded onto aircraft, Burma.

In January 1942, when the Japanese invaded Burma, the British War Office offered General Wavell, Commander-in-Chief India, the services of Lieutenant-Colonel Orde Wingate, D.S.O. and bar, who had previously carried out guerrilla operations in Palestine and Abyssinia with conspicuous success. Wavell, under whom Wingate had served, recognised his excellent if unorthodox qualities, saw a rôle for him in Burma, and accepted this offer.

On Wingate's arrival in India after the fall of Rangoon, Wavell sent him to carry out a reconnaissance in north Burma, which he thought might be suitable terrain for guerrillas. Wingate flew in and was conducted around north Burma by the commandant of the Bush Warfare School at Maymyo, Major J. M. Calvert, who

was later to join him. Calvert also motored Wingate south some hundreds of miles to Prome to meet Lieutenant-General Slim, commander of I Burma Corps. This corps had only just been formed, after the fall of Rangoon.

After a detailed reconnaissance and after discussing the matter with many people, including Chiang Kai-shek in Chungking, Wingate returned to India.

He reported to Wavell that at that juncture there were neither time nor troops available to form a pattern of guerrilla warfare in north Burma, but he did recommend forming and training a special force of brigade strength, which could penetrate behind the Japanese forces and destroy their communications and perhaps manoeuvre them out of the area.

Wavell's dilemma, and his final decision

Originally the raid planned for the seven Chindit columns, each of about 400 men and 100 mules with two 3-inch mortars and two medium machine guns, was to be supported by a general offensive by IV Corps from Imphal. But IV Corps' (Scoones) communications were not ready, and so it was reluctant to advance across the Chindwin in any strength. Wavell, however, was determined that this experimental brigade should test out not only the Japanese but these new means of operating in the deep jungle. Wavell came forward to Imphal, inspected the 77th Brigade and, after deep thought, directed it into the attack alone. Wavell had had to consider whether the risk of losing all or part of this brigade on a mission of little strategic value, in order to attempt to burst the bubble of Japanese invincibility, would be balanced by the experience gained and the loss of technical surprise when such tactics had to be used later to support a general offensive. He finally decided that it was worth the risk, because the operation would help raise morale in the army in India, by showing that Allied forces could operate in jungle terrain and need not feel inferior to the Japanese in fighting along unconventional lines.

Gurkhas move into action

On February 14 the headquarters and three British and four Gurkha columns of the 77th Brigade successfully crossed the Chindwin and advanced secretly on a broad front through the jungle-covered hills into central Burma. Their objective was the main north-south Burma railway between Mandalay and Mogaung. The distance from their starting point to the railway direct was about 140 miles. Major Dunlop's No. 1 (Gurkha) Column was the first to reach the railway on March 3 when it destroyed railway bridges near Kyaikthin. No. 3 (Gurkha) Column (Calvert) did the same 40 miles north at Nankan on the night March 5–6. No. 5 (King's) Column (Fergusson) on the same night brought down an avalanche of rock onto the railway in the Bongyaung (Bonchaung) Gorge. The forces taking part in this operation totalled about 3,000 men and 800 mules.

The Japanese 18th and 33rd divisions of the 15th Army, under Lieutenant-General Iida, were the formations most affected by this raid, and for a while they were bewildered by it. They did not take the situation seriously until Dunlop (Royal Scots) blew the railway on March 3. Then Iida ordered three regiments, each of three battalions, to round up the raiders.

Wingate, however, exalted by this first success, ordered his columns to cross the 1,000-yard wide Irrawaddy. He envisaged forming a base in the friendly Kachin Hills to the north-east, from where he could operate with his back to the Chinese during the next few months. But he also ordered Calvert and Fergusson to attack the Burma Road in the Maymyo area, where the Japanese headquarters were situated and therefore where the maximum reaction to the raid would result.

First defeat

But one of the Gurkha columns had already met with disaster when approaching the railway, and had been dispersed. The news of this spread to the other Gurkha columns and it became more difficult to keep up their morale. It should be explained that whilst the Gurkhas, when properly trained and with officers who speak their language, are magnificent troops, they naturally cannot so easily change the tactics and methods taught them at their depots at short notice as can, for example, British troops, who understood the language in which the new concepts of such tactics are taught. The Gurkha battalion given to Wingate for this operation was woefully short of experienced officers and men, and only about one officer in each column spoke Gurkhali well. In Calvert's column, for instance, only one British officer with the Gurkha company was over the age of 19. It is all the more remarkable that these young officers led their fine young men, assisted by excellent Gurkhali warrant officers and N.C.O.s, through nearly three months of operations in the jungle without cracking.

The crossing of the Irrawaddy was not easy and more than one column was attacked whilst carrying out this difficult manoeuvre. Perhaps the crossing was a mistake. After their initial rapid march and successful demolitions, the Chindits found themselves hemmed in between the Irrawaddy and the Shweli rivers in a dry inhospitable area with no nearby targets to attack and at the extreme range of their wireless sets and air supply communications. The Japanese used regiments from three (18th, 33rd, 56th) of their four divisions in Burma at that time to try to surround and destroy the Chindits.

Many small actions were fought until the time came when Wingate, after radio consultation with IV Corps, decided to withdraw his force. He ordered his column commanders to try to bring back their columns complete into India or to take them on to China. He gave them the alternative option of splitting into dispersal groups as taught in training, so that they might infiltrate between the strands of the Japanese net which was now surrounding them. One King's column (Gilkes) chose the longer, more arduous, but safer route to China. Another King's column, under Scott, who had been a Royal Engineer, chose to make an airstrip in an open space in the jungle and be flown out from the other side of the Irrawaddy. The remainder recrossed the Irrawaddy either in dispersal groups or columns and made their way back to the Chindwin. Unfortunately many of them thought they were safe on reaching the Chindwin, but IV Corps had withdrawn from it and the Japanese were now using it as a stop line to catch the Chindit columns in that area. The result was that many prisoners were taken on the Chindwin itself, when the dispersal group thought that it had reached safe harbour and had relaxed.

Of the 3,000 men and 800 mules which had crossed the Chindwin, about 2,182 men and two mules returned, having covered between 1,000 and 1,500 miles in enemy-dominated territory. The remainder had been killed, captured, or if mules, eaten. But those who returned, although suffering from malaria, dysentery, jungle sores, and malnutrition, were in high spirits and proud of their achievement. Sent on leave and supported by a well-directed public relations campaign in the press, they had a startling effect on the raising of morale of all ranks throughout India, especially at that time when the defeats in the Arakan had

Bombers attack Japanese stores and supply depots, Burma.

further depressed men's minds. There they were, ordinary second line battalions and anything but picked troops, but they had gone through Burma and "singed Tojo's moustache". So their comrades in units throughout India and Assam said "if that lot can run rings round the Japanese we can do better".

Imphal idea born

This the first Chindit operation was the direct begetter of Mutaguchi's "U-Go" offensive against the 14th Army at Imphal in March 1944. This operation, after achieving initial success, failed because failed because Mutaguchi had apparently not understood that the vital necessity for such an operation was dominance of the air, and consequent reliable air supply and close air support in lieu of artillery.

Much has been made of the divergencies of opinion amongst the Allies on how they should conduct the war against Japan, but one decision made in 1943 stands out plainly. At the Combined Chiefs-of-Staff "Quadrant" Conference in Quebec in August 1943, which Brigadier Wingate attended at Churchill's request, it was decided "To carry out operations for the capture of upper Burma in order to improve the air route and establish overland communications with China. Our main effort should be put into offensive operations to achieve this object."

In order to achieve this result the British Chiefs-of-Staff decided to form six Long Range Penetration Groups (L.R.P.G.), which would conduct operations as outlined by Brigadier Wingate and enable the Allies to seize sufficient of north Burma to open a road to China.

These six L.R.P. brigades would each consist of four battalions and attached troops. The force, which was known variously as the Special Force, the 3rd Indian Infantry Division (as a cover name), or the Chindits, would consist of two Indian infantry brigades (77th and 111th) already in being; three brigades formed from the battle-experienced British 70th Division; and one brigade formed from the 81st West African Division. The three battalions of this African brigade would be available to this force to act as garrisons for the air bases formed in the jungle to support each brigade.

These bases, which Wingate called "strongholds", were what the modern tactician tends to call "pivots of manoeuvre".

A One of six officers and men of the Kings Regiment on the first expedition in 1943 is decorated bv Lord Wauell, Viceroy of India. Fergusson admitted that the Chindits had not achieved a

great deal, though they had distracted the Japanese from some operations. However, they had "amassed experience on which a future has already begun to be built". Wingate went home and captured the imagination of both Churchill and Roosevelt.

To support China

At the "Sextant" Conference held in Cairo in November 1943, which Chiang Kai-shek attended, the Combined Chiefs-of-Staff ordered "the occupation of Upper Burma by the Allies to start in February 1944 in order to improve (a) the air and (b) the land routes to China. What was attempted elsewhere in Asia would be in support of this main effort."

The main reason for the Allies giving this plan of operations top priority was the real fear that, unless the British and Americans opened up even such tenuous communications to China in the manner projected, China would drop out of the war and thus allow the 26 Japanese divisions operating in China to be used elsewhere against the Allies. It is important that this agreed plan of action by the Allies should be borne in mind throughout all discussions on this campaign, because future operations by either side as the battlefield spread, tended to blur the horizon and deflect certain commanders' minds away from the maintenance of this objective which had been laid down by the inter-Allied high command.

CHRONOLOGY OF WORLD WAR II

	1938
March 11	Anschluss — German annexation of Austria.
September 29	Munich Agreement signed.
October 5	Germany occupies Sudetenland.
	1939
March 14	Slovakia declares its independence.
March 31	Britain and France give guarantee to Poland.
April 7	Italy invades Albania.
May 22	Germany and Italy sign Pact of Steel.
August 23	Molotov-Ribbentrop pact signed between Germany and the Soviet Union.
September 1	Germany invades Poland.
September 1	Britain and France declare war on Germany.
September 17	Soviet Union invades Poland.
November 30	Soviet Union at war with Finland.
	1940
March 12	War between Soviet Union and Finland ends.
April 9	Germany invades Norway and Denmark.
April 14	Allied troops land in Norway.
May 10	Fall Gelb, the offensive in the West, is launched by Germany.
May 10	Churchill becomes Prime Minister of Great Britain.
May 14	Dutch Army surrenders.
May 26	Beginning of evacuation of Dunkirk.
May 28	Belgium surrenders.
June 2	Allies withdraw from Norway.
June 4	Dunkirk evacuation complete.
June 10	Italy declares war on Britain and France.
June 14	Germans enter Paris.
June 21	Italy launches offensive against France.
June 22	France and Germany sign armistice.
June 24	France and Italy sign armistice.
July 3	Royal Navy attacks French fleet at Mers el Kebir.
July 10	Beginning of the Battle of Britain.
September 17	Operation Sealion (the invasion of England) postponed by Hitler.
September 21	Italy and Germany sign Tripartite Pact.
September 27	Japan signs Tripartite Pact.
November 20	Hungary signs Tripartite Pact.
November 22	Romania signs Tripartite Pact.
November 23	Slovakia signs Tripartite Pact.
	1941
January 19	British launch East African campaign offensive.
January 22	Australian troops take Tobruk.
February 6	British capture Benghazi.
February 11	Rommel arrives in Libya.

March 25	Yugoslavia signs Tripartite Pact.
March 27	Yugoslavia leaves Tripartite Pact after coup d'etat.
March 28	Successful British naval action against Italians off Cape Matapan.
April 6–8	Axis forces invade Yugoslavia and Greece.
April 11	U.S.A. extends its naval neutrality patrols.
April 13	Belgrade falls to Axis forces.
April 14	Yugoslav forces surrender.
April 22	Greek First Army surrenders at Metsovan Pass.
May 16	Italians surrender to British at Amba Alagi.
May 20	Germans land on Crete.
May 24	H.M.S. Hood sunk by Bismarck.
May 27	Bismarck sunk by Royal Navy.
June 1	British withdraw from Crete.
June 2	Germany launches Operation Barbarossa against the Soviet Union.
July 27	Japanese troops invade French Indo-China.
September 19	Germans capture Kiev.
September 28	Three-power Conference in Moscow.
December 6	Britain declares war on Finland, Hungary and Rumania.
December 7	Japanese attack Pearl Harbor.
December 8	U.S.A. and Britain declare war on Japan.
December 8	Japanese invade Malaya and Thailand.
December 11	Germany and Italy declare war on the U.S.A.
December 14	Japanese begin invasion of Burma.
December 25	Japanese take Hong Kong.
1942	
February 15	Japanese troops capture Singapore from British.
February 27	Battle of the Java Sea.
February 28	Japanese invade Java.
March 8	Japanese invade New Guinea.
March 17	General MacArthur appointed to command South-West Pacific.
April 9	U.S. troops surrender in Bataan.
April 16	George Cross awarded to Island of Malta by H.R.H. King George VI.
April 26	Anglo-Soviet Treaty signed.
May 6	Japanese take Corregidor.
May 7	Battle of the Coral Sea.
May 20	British troops withdraw from Burma.
May 26	Rommel's Afrika Korps attack British at Gazala.
May 30	Royal Air Force launches first thousand-bomber raid on Germany.
June 4	Battle of Midway.
June 21	Rommel's Afrika Korps take Tobruk.
July 1	Sevastopol taken by Germans.
July 1	First Battle of El Alamein.
August 7	U.S. troops land on Guadalcanal.
August 11	PEDESTAL convoy arrives in Malta.
August 19	Raid on Dieppe.

August 31	Battle of Alam Halfa.
October 24	Second Battle of El Alamein.
November 8	Operation TORCH landings in North Africa.
November 11	Germans and Italians occupy Vichy France.
November 27	French fleet scuttled at Toulon.
1943	
January 14–24	Allied Conference at Casablanca.
January 23	British troops take Tripoli.
February 2	Germans surrender at Stalingrad.
February 8	Red Army captures Kursk.
February 13	Chindits launch first operation into Burma.
February 19	Battle for the Kasserine Pass.
April 19	First Warsaw rising.
April 19	Bermuda Conference.
May 11–25	TRIDENT conference in Washington.
May 13	Axis forces surrender in North Africa.
May 16	Royal Air Force "Dambuster" raid on Mohne and Eder dams.
May 24	U-boats withdraw from North Atlantic.
July 5	Battle of Kursk.
July 10	Allies land in Sicily.
July 25	Mussolini resigns.
September 3	Allies land on Italian mainland.
September 8	Surrender of Italy announced.
September 9	Allies land at Salerno.
September 10	Germans occupy Rome and Northern Italy.
October 13	Italy declares war on Germany.
November 6	Red Army captures Kiev.
November	First Allied conference in Cairo. 23–26
November 28–December 1	Allied conference in Teheran.
December 3–7	Second Allied conference in Cairo.
December 24	General Eisenhower promoted to supreme commander for OVERLORD, the Normandy landings.
1944	
January 22	Allies land at Anzio.
January 27	Red Army raises Siege of Leningrad.
January 31	U.S. forces land on Marshall Islands.
February 1	Battle for Monte Cassino begins.
March 2	Second Chindit operation into Burma.
May 11	Fourth Battle of Monte Cassino.
June 4	U.S. troops enter Rome.
June 6	Operation OVERLORD — Allied landings in Normandy.
June 19	Battle of the Philippine Sea.
July 1	Breton Woods conference.
July 20	Failed attempt to assassinate Hitler — July Bomb plot.
August 1	Second Warsaw rising.
August 4	Allied troops enter Florence.

August 15	Operation DRAGOON — Allied landings in southern France.
August 25	Germans in Paris surrender.
September 4	British troops capture Antwerp.
September	OCTAGON — Allied conference at Quebec. 12–16
September 17	Operation MARKET GARDEN at Arnhem.
September 21	Dumbarton Oaks conference.
October 14	British enter Athens.
October 23	De Gaulle recognised by Britain and U.S.A. as head of French Provisional Government.
October 24	Battle of Leyte Gulf.
December 16	Germans launch campaign in the Ardennes.
1945	
January 4–13	Japanese Kamikaze planes sink 17 U.S. ships and damage 50 more.
January 14	Red Army advances into East Prussia.
January 17	Red Army takes Warsaw.
January 30–February 3	First ARGONAUT Allied conference at Malta.
February 4–11	Second ARGONAUT Allied conference at Malta.
February 6	Allies clear Colmar pocket.
February 19	U.S. forces land on Iwo Jima.
February 26	U.S. 9th Army reaches Rhine.
March 7	U.S. 3rd Army crosses Rhine at Remagen Bridge.
March 20	British capture Mandalay.
March 30	Red Army enters Austria.
April 1	U.S. First and Ninth Armies encircle the Ruhr.
April 1	U.S. forces land on Okinawa.
April 12	President Roosevelt dies and Truman becomes president.
April 13	Red Army takes Vienna.
April 25	U.S. and Soviet forces meet at Torgau.
April 28	Mussolini shot by partisans.
April 29	Germans sign surrender terms for troops in Italy.
April 30	Hitler commits suicide.
May 2	Red Army takes Berlin.
May 3	British enter Rangoon.
May 4	German forces in the Netherlands, northern Germany and Denmark surrender to General Montgomery on Luneburg Heath.
May 5	Germans in Norway surrender.
May 7	General Alfred Jodl signs unconditional surrender of Germany at Reims, to take effect on May 9.
May 8	Victory in Europe Day.
May 10	Red Army takes Prague.
July 17–August 2	Allied TERMINAL conference held in Potsdam.
July 26	Winston Churchill resigns after being defeated in the general election. Clement Attlee becomes Prime Minister of Great Britain.
August 6	Atomic bomb dropped on Hiroshima.
August 8	Soviet Union declares war on Japan.
August 9	Atomic bomb dropped on Nagasaki.
August 14	Unconditional surrender of Japanese forces announced by Emperor Hirohito.
August 15	Victory in Japan Day.
September 2	Japanese sign surrender aboard U.S.S. Missouri in Tokyo Bay.